The Deep South in Transformation

THE DEEP SOUTH IN TRANSFORMATION

A Symposium

EDITED BY ROBERT B. HIGHSAW

UNIVERSITY OF ALABAMA PRESS

UNIVERSITY·ALABAMA

Library of Congress Catalog Card Number: 64-25846
Manufactured in the United States of America
by Kingsport Press, Inc., Kingsport, Tennessee
Designed by Klaus Gemming

FOREWORD

THE TITLE given this volume of essays and commentaries asserts confidently that the Deep South is in transformation. It raises two questions: What is the Deep South? What transformation is occurring? Neither question is easy to answer precisely and definitively, although replies to both frequently are assumed implicitly by many people who write of the region and its problems.

Still, a specific geographical location must be given when a region embracing many sub-regions, as Howard Odum pointed out a generation ago, is the subject of a series of essays and commentaries. It is to be accepted as a fact that there are many Souths, but for our purposes the Deep South embraces Alabama, Florida, Georgia, Louisiana, Mississippi, and South Carolina. This area is much smaller than that of the Confederate South, which included additionally Arkansas, North Carolina, Tennessee, Texas, and Virginia. Both are still smaller than the United States Bureau of the Census' South, which includes within the region as well Delaware, the District of Columbia, Kentucky, Maryland, Oklahoma, and West Virginia. Any of the three descriptions is somewhat arbitrary and unsatisfactory; certainly Dallas and Birmingham, Atlanta and Baltimore, New Orleans and Boston have a sharper affinity with each other than they have with rural places within their respective states.

There may well be more to describing a region, or subregion, than the imposition of geographical boundaries. For example, one of the commentators in this book suggests that there is presently no identifiable Deep South except that which might be defined as a state of mind. Even in this sense there is no unanimity. The literature of the region has given contrasting and sometimes unrealistic views of the Deep South. In them geography is unimportant. One picture paints a land of moonlight and magnolias, of meandering rivers and the wealth of endless fields of cotton, of gentle and sweet womanhood and gallant and courageous men, and of loyal and enduring Negroes. The other draws the grim lines of racial violence and moral ruin, of wayward women and degenerate men, and of relentless and implacable poverty. The Deep South, indeed the entire South, has both men of tolerance and men of intolerance, men of honor and men without honor; it has the sharp contrasts of wealth and poverty, of progressivism and reaction, of education and ignorance. The social point of view is complex, but not without foundation. The differences between the Deep South states, on the one hand, and the Confederate South and the Census South, on the other, are largely ones of degree. Indeed, much of the difference between the three Souths and the nation as a whole can be similarly defined. All the delimitation of the Deep South to six states does, of course, is to give a convenient, though by no means rigid, frame of reference.

The answer to the second question, what transformation is occurring in the Deep South, is quite a different one. A transformation occurs when there is a change in external form or in inner nature or function. And in this sense the Deep South is transforming, or changing, or emerging into a new area. A few empirical trends offer ample evidence of this conclusion.

For example, census statistics indicate that the population of the Deep South continues to grow less rapidly than that of the United States. Although Florida's annual rate of population change showed an increase of 6.0 per cent 1950-1960, Alabama's rose yearly only 0.7 per cent, Georgia's 1.4 per cent, Louisiana's 2.0 per cent, Mississippi's none, and South

Carolina's 1.4 per cent. In the same decade, Negro population changes showed a net loss of 33 per cent in Mississippi and a substantial gain in Florida and Louisiana among the Deep South states. Net migration of both whites and Negroes is responsible chiefly for slow population growth in the Deep South. Every state in the region has had a net non-white out-migration in the last twenty years, and all except Florida and Louisiana, which attracted whites in the 1950's, have lost white migrants.

These population figures reflect an economic response as well as a reaction to population pressure. Although per capita income in the Deep South, relative to the national average, is higher than it was thirty years ago, the 1960 per capita income in Mississippi was only 53 per cent of the national average. The other five states of the region showed substantial relative increases when 1960's figures were compared with 1929's. Alabama had a 1960 per capita income of 66 per cent of the national average compared to only 46 per cent in 1929; Georgia had 72 per cent compared to 50 per cent for the same period; Florida had 89 per cent compared to 74 per cent; South Carolina had 63 per cent versus 38 per cent; and Louisiana had 72 per cent compared to 59 per cent. These percentages make for dull reading, but they are significant because they denote changing activity in the Deep South, a relative increase in manufacturing and a similar decrease in agriculture. The expansion of manufacturing and industrial activity, therefore, appears to be the most important means for enlarging the economic base of the Deep South. Indeed, this fact has been long known, and there is hardly a southern governor, or candidate for governor, who does not press the industrialization of his state. Henry Grady's *New South* is not only respectable doctrine; it is revered dogma.

The growth record of manufacturing and industrial activities in the Deep South readily provides an explanation for this reverence. Manufacturing employment, 1958 compared to 1929, increased 73 per cent in Alabama, 135 per cent in Florida, 83 per cent in Georgia, 40 per cent in Louisiana, 92 per cent in Mississippi, and 96 per cent in South Carolina. Visibly, people in the Deep South are more concerned with manufacturing than before; this concern is evidenced by the physical plants that dot even the open country of Alabama, Georgia, Mississippi, and South Carolina. Economic growth is related, however, to some limiting factors: to adjustment to changes in market demand, to technological innovations, to composition of the labor force, and to others. These factors have led some observers to conclude that four Deep South states—Alabama, Georgia, Mississippi, and South Carolina—have a potentially unfavorable position, while the competitive position of Louisiana is potentially superior to them and that of Florida is even better than Louisiana's.

Meanwhile, the people of the Deep South have been on the move, from the rural areas to the villages and towns and from them to the metropolitan areas of the region. By the 1960 census Alabama was 54 per cent urban, Florida 73 per cent, Georgia 55 per cent, and Louisiana 63 per cent; only South Carolina, with 41 per cent urban population, and Mississippi, with 37 per cent, were predominantly rural. The impact of this move toward urbanization is reflected in the fact that, compared to only seven metropolitan areas in the Deep South in 1930, there were twenty-eight in 1960. To the familiar names of Atlanta, Birmingham, and New Orleans, to cite three, were added such areas as Augusta, Georgia, Baton Rouge, Louisiana, Huntsville, Alabama, and Pensacola, Florida.

The development of manufacturing and the accompanying trend toward urbanization created a need for organizing more effective government at the state and local levels. This need has been only partially met. Four of the six state governments—Mississippi and South Carolina are the exceptions—have undergone substantial administrative reorganizations. The reapportioning of state legislative bodies to give fair representation to urban areas began only under federal court order and has not yet reached full fruition. Only in a few isolated instances has much been done to improve county structures and processes—the traditional local, rural institutions of government. Florida, Georgia, and South Carolina have moved rapidly into the council-manager plan for cities, but Alabama, Louisiana, and Mississippi have made little progress in re-structuring for urban problems. Miami and Nashville have sought to adjust governmental structures to urbanization and metropolitanism in a striking new fashion. Change has been, at best, spotty and reflects the fact that governmental innovations and newer and more effective governmental processes require departure from a traditional absence of concern about social responsibility.

Population change, economic development, and governmental innovation all are affected by cultural patterns, and here we encounter what historians of the region have called the "central theme"—the Negro in the Deep South. No longer can we agree with Will Percy, who, in his *Lanterns on the Levee* (1941), expressed "amazed exultation over the excellent state of race relations in the South." Implicit in several of the essays of this volume is recognition that the Negro in the Deep South is in revolution in the 1960's, and equally implicit is the recognition that in relatively few cases has the white southerner agreed to estrange himself from the familiar cultural patterns of the Deep South's plural society. It is this which has led Leslie W. Dunbar of the Southern Regional Council to remark—perhaps with bitterness, perhaps with sadness—that the "white South is an object, and only subjects can, even in a Faulknerian sense, endure."*

This Deep South, this disturbed and troubled region, is the subject of this volume. If the social heritage of the Deep South has developed a truculent pride in local customs and traditions, if it has produced extreme resistance to external criticism, it is also true that emotional associations which have any intellectually analyzable meaning slowly change. Yet much change is being effected in the Deep South by local decisions, and with these decisions habits also alter. We may yet come to accept the eloquent words of Mr. Justice Oliver Wendell Holmes that

> . . . when men realize that time has upset many fighting faiths, they may come to believe even more than they believe the very foundations of their conduct that the ultimate good desired is better reached by free trade in ideas—that the best test of truth is the power of the thought to get itself accepted in the competition of the market, and that truth is the only ground upon which their wishes safely can be carried out. That at any rate is the theory of our Constitution.†

Today the Deep South stands, as it undergoes transformation, in the market of ideas.

The essays and commentaries that follow this foreword were delivered at the Conference on the Social Sciences and the Development of the Deep South, held on the University of Alabama campus April 23-25, 1964. This conference was sponsored by the University faculties of history, philosophy, political science, and sociology-anthropology in honor of the dedication of a new social sciences building, Marten ten

* "The Changing Mind of the South: The Exposed Nerve," *Journal of Politics*, February, 1964, 8.

† Dissenting opinion in *Abrams* v. *United States*, 250 U.S. 616, 630-31 (1919).

Hoor Hall. The faculties were joined in sponsorship by the Southeastern American Studies Association and by the Sperry and Hutchinson College Lectureship Program. Grateful acknowledgment must be made of the generous grant-in-aid from the Sperry and Hutchinson Company, which helped to make the conference possible.

Appreciation must be expressed to Frank A. Rose, President of the University of Alabama, whose deep interest in the program and in the social sciences removed many an obstacle. Dean Frederick W. Conner, College of Arts and Sciences; the Social Science Building Committee, Charles Grayson Summersell, Chairman; and Professor Clarence C. Mondale, Director of American Studies, were charged with planning the conference; to them thanks are given. Material assistance in the many details arising from such a meeting was provided by Willard Van Brown, Assistant to the President for University Relations, and Charles E. Adams, Coordinator of Conference Activities. The merit of the volume rests with the speakers and with the quality of ideas presented by them.

Robert B. Highsaw

July 1, 1964
University, Alabama

CONTRIBUTORS

CARL BENSON, now a member of the Auburn University faculty, has taught also at the Arkansas Agricultural and Mechanical College and the University of Illinois.

JOHN W. BLOOMER, a southern editor and publisher since 1935, is Managing Editor of the *Birmingham News.*

OLIVER C. CARMICHAEL, former Chancellor of Vanderbilt University and former President of Alabama College, has been also President of the Carnegie Foundation for the Advancement of Teaching and served as the eighteenth President of the University of Alabama.

JOHN S. EZELL has been Chairman of the Department of History at the University of Oklahoma since 1962.

FRANK FREIDEL, now Professor of History at Harvard University and Chairman of the Committee on Higher Degrees in the History of American Civilization, also was Harmsworth Professor of American History at Oxford University 1955-56.

ROBERT B. HIGHSAW, currently a member of the Council of the American Society for Public Administration, is Professor and Head, Department of Political Science, and Director of the Bureau of Public Administration at the University of Alabama.

LUTHER H. HODGES, former Governor of North Carolina, has been United States Secretary of Commerce since 1961.

PHILIP G. HOFFMAN, formerly a member of the faculty of the University of Alabama, since 1961 has been President of the University of Houston.

EVERETT C. HUGHES, Professor of Sociology at Brandeis University and past President of the American Sociological Association, is the co-editor of *Race: Individual and Collective Behavior*, published in 1958.

ERNEST M. LANDER, JR., author of *A History of South Carolina, 1865-1960*, is Professor of History and Government at Clemson College.

JAMES L. MILLER, JR., frequently a consultant to state studies of higher education, has been Associate Director for Research, Southern Regional Education Board since 1962.

E. WILLIAM NOLAND, now Professor and Head, Department of Sociology at Purdue University, was Chairman of the Division of Social Sciences, University of North Carolina 1956-62.

REMBERT W. PATRICK, President of the Southern Historical Association in 1962 and now Julien C. Yonge Graduate Research Professor of History at the University of Florida, was awarded the Bohnenberger Medal for his volume, *Jefferson Davis and His Cabinet*.

LOUIS D. RUBIN, JR., Professor of English and Chairman of the Department at Hollins College, has had extensive teaching experience, has written one novel and several critical studies, and was formerly editor of the *Hopkins Review*.

HUDSON STRODE, author and lecturer, is now Professor Emeritus of English at the University of Alabama.

DONALD S. STRONG, long an observer of the southern political scene, has been Professor of Political Science, University of Alabama, since 1952 and a member of the faculty since 1946.

WALTER L. SULLIVAN, Professor of English at Vanderbilt University, is well known as a novelist, literary critic, and essayist.

MARTEN TEN HOOR, now Dean Emeritus of the College of Arts and Sciences and Professor Emeritus of Philosophy at the University of Alabama, has been also Dean at Tulane University and was formerly Chairman of the Council of the Oak Ridge Institute of Nuclear Studies.

CONTENTS

THE DEEP SOUTH IN TRANSFORMATION

Prologue

Marten ten Hoor

The Social Sciences in Higher Education

It is the privilege of a dean emeritus gently but firmly to disavow any responsibility for the academic activities which go on, and will continue for a long time to go on, in his University and for their educational consequences. But this is not intended, even by the most subtle implication, to suggest that I am not interested in these matters. Underlying the basic subject of the social sciences and the development of the Deep South is the broader problem of the role of the social sciences, and of the humanities also, in contemporary higher education. This is a subject in which I have been long interested and officially deeply involved. In presenting some reflections on the subject, I am not attempting to offer solutions, but only to mention some problems, procedural problems at that. In short, I am seeking light, not undertaking to spread it.

The problems, long-standing ones, have become recently more complex and more acute, principally because of their current setting, namely, the steadily growing emphasis which, from necessity or choice, is being laid on the natural sciences. Today education, and particularly higher education, is being subjected to influences which in themselves lie outside of the area of formal education, in events and conditions in the outside world. The occurrence of such pressure is nothing new in the long-term history of education. Whenever society stakes its faith on some subject matter area, various kinds and degrees of pressure are directed at the institutions responsible for formal education. The dominance of theology, classical humanism, and Baconian scientific empiricism are familiar examples. It is true that we are not always able to determine accurately the original or moving cause of these pressures, for sometimes these shifts of emphasis are the result of gradual changes in interests and emphases and commitments of the educators themselves. In the current situation, we can feel certain that international political developments, and in consequence military necessities, have been the principal source of this demand for emphasis upon the natural sciences, although there has lately been a gradual but steady shift to interest in, and occupation with, this kind of knowledge for its own sake, that is to say, towards the pure science approach.

The resultant outcropping in professional and lay circles of a demand for more emphasis upon the humanities and the social sciences is in part a defense reaction. Fortunately it has not been merely a defensive but also an offensive one, the latter taking the form of a critical re-analysis of the contribution which these two groups of subjects can make to the education of the American citizen for participation in the solution of the domestic and foreign problems by which we are these days beset. It is fortunate also that the approach of the proponents of these subjects has been judicious, with an occasional exception. What is required in the current circumstances is a calm and objective analysis of the potentialities of these subjects, accompanied by such proof as can be reasonably expected. I say reasonably expected because of the inherent limitations of the educational enterprise per se, and, to be sure, of the human beings engaged in it. What I have in mind is indicated, though with some exaggeration, in an addition to an old saying: To the time-worn saw that

"Doctors bury their mistakes" and an earlier addendum "And lawyers leave them hanging," is the charge, "And professors never discover them." Surely, the most embarrassing response one can receive to insistence upon the educational effects of a subject in the areas of the humanities and the social sciences is the demand to "prove it." This is especially the case when some specific claim is made; for some degree of safety is assured if the claim is a general one, e.g., that "mankind will ultimately benefit from it."

Fortunately, I have now for about four years been in a rather comfortable position to reflect on these matters. I have had the time but not the responsibility to prove anything. The first conclusion of my reflections is that we proponents of these subjects have been somewhat handicapped by our educational inheritance. There is first of all the matter of names and the meanings which have come to be attached to them. In the case of the term "humanities" we have, more or less unwittingly, come to take for granted that any subject so named, and any part of that subject, has more human value than subjects not so named. To be sure, we have not gone so far as to consider other subjects "inhumanities," but we have privately and publicly assumed an attitude of moral superiority. We have forgotten that historically the name reports a reaction of our educational ancestors to an overemphasis upon the sacred science, theology. We still hear faint echoes of this in the current disputes between theologians and secular humanists.

We have also forgotten that the social sciences were originally a reaction to specific limitations of the humanities. To be sure, the social scientists, even the most enthusiastic, have not gone so far as to consider, or at least publicly to characterize, the humanities as anti- or asocial; but they have been inclined to feel that their importance was overemphasized. It cannot be denied that some of the scholarly undertakings of the humanists, for example, the exhumation of a fifth-rate Latin, or French, or English poet, cannot be said to have much social value. In fact, it can be said to have private value only for the scholar. But it can always be argued that this makes at least one man happy and possibly entertains some of his colleagues, and is thus a social gain, though a minor one. Moreover, compared with the collection of money or power, it is quite an innocent one.

The first point to make here is that, in this matter of evaluation of the subjects in the curriculum, we have been somewhat misled by the habit of defining by classification and thus substituting classification for critical analysis. We have a good example in the case of Marten ten Hoor Hall. From the beginning this structure has been referred to as the Social Sciences Building. In consequence, students, and even faculty members in sister colleges, have been led to assume that all departments and all of the subjects domiciled in the building were social sciences. This is not justified even by the principle of majority rule. For of the four departments in the building two, namely history and philosophy, have been traditionally included among the humanities. This matter may be in part a reflection of the fact that, in the College of Arts and Sciences here at Alabama, history and philosophy are included in a group of courses from which the student must select two in order to satisfy the social science requirement for graduation. To be sure, in placing these two subjects in this group the faculty had no intention of designating them as social sciences. This was purely a marriage of convenience. In the case of philosophy one member of the faculty is said to have commented that it was a counsel of despair.

My second point is that there is too easy and uncritical use and implied acceptance of the old Commencement Address favorite that "the natural sciences are concerned with facts and the humanities and the social sciences with values." The superficiality and inherent inaccuracy of this statement is obvious. Thus, the existence or nonexistence of a value is itself a fact. The establishment that a specific value should or should not be pursued by human beings is either a matter of fact or merely a matter of taste or fancy, and is thus, in the last analysis, also a matter of fact. In the case of the logician, for example, ways of right and wrong thinking are facts and so are their consequences and the uses which can be made of them. Witness the politicians. The methods of the literary scholar, of the psychologist, of the social analyst, and so forth, therefore must to some extent be basically the same as those of the natural scientist. Finally, the natural sciences cannot properly be said to be unconcerned with values. Scientific inquiry is conducted by and for human beings. Technologies are devised by human beings for the use of other human beings. The fact that scientists insist that scientific inquiry must not be limited a priori by anticipation of use or non-use is itself a value judgment. But modern scientists have ventured even farther into the realm of values. At least some of them, including some world figures, have taken the position that when scientists reveal discoveries and techniques to the world which can be used for destructive purposes they must bear some of the responsibility for such use. The insistence by another group that to conceal destructive uses means running the risk of exposing supposedly good men to the power of evil men is also a value judgment.

My third point is that the categorical distinction between facts and values will not stand up even when applied within the boundaries of a humanities or social science department. In the case of philosophy, for example, there is a great difference between a course in logic and a course in the history of philosophy in respect to comparative emphasis upon fact and value. The same is true for a course in grammar and a course in literary history. In fact, courses in grammar and logic closely resemble courses in technology in the area of the natural sciences.

My fourth point makes confusion worse confounded. Let us not forget that there are courses in some professional curricula which are partially or wholly concerned with professional ethics, that is to say, values, and with conflicts between professional moral standards and those of the communities in which the profession is to function.

It is clear that we cannot make across-the-board distinctions such as we are accustomed to make in everyday discussion, in faculty meetings, and in college bulletins. Granted that this is the case, by what rules or principles ought we to be guided in making particular distinctions? Personally, I have found it helpful to do this, insofar as classroom instruction is concerned, in terms of three fundamental purposes of education. These are: (1) The transmission of factual knowledge in the field with which the subject is concerned. We call this "pure" science. (2) The transmission of knowledge concerning the proven and possible uses of such factual knowledge, that is, technological knowledge. (3) The transmission of opinions or convictions, based on human experience, as to how this technological knowledge ought to be used. This is the realm of human values per se and might be given the name of human wisdom.

That the last named kind of knowledge is involved in formal education, directly or by implication, is obvious. Bacon was correct in affirming that "knowledge is power." But it would have been better if he had added "for good or for evil." The politician who has a knowledge of the fallacies, especially of the subtle ones, can use this knowledge, either to enlighten or mislead the public. The Madison Avenue public relations expert can use knowledge of human psychology to misrepresent the qualities of the products or the intentions of the people he represents. We are told that by using the latest refinements of psychological techniques we can be influenced on television without being aware of the fact that we are actually listening to a commercial.

For the sake of the argument, assume that instruction in pure science and technology presents no particularly difficult or complex problems and that, in our modern institutions of higher education, it is competent and adequate. But what about the transmission of what we shall continue to call, for lack of a better term, moral wisdom? Should this be transmitted in courses in the humanities and the social sciences, and if so, how?

It is clear that in trying to answer this question we must take into consideration four variables which are involved in the enterprise of education: the subject matter, the professor, the student, and the environing society. In the case of the subject matter, there are two ways in which variation can occur: (1) the difference between subjects in respect to inherent emphasis upon facts, techniques, and values; and (2) developments in a subject matter which result in changes of such emphases. However, the inherent differences and developments can be fairly easily identified by careful analysis and do not, therefore, in themselves, present any serious problem.

The second variable, the professor, presents a far different problem. First of all, he can establish his own emphases, even to the extent of changing the inherent objectives of the course which he is teaching. Secondly, we come face-to-face here with sharply opposed opinions with respect to the extent to which a professor should concern himself with expressing opinions or convictions as to how the knowledge which he transmits should be used by mankind. There are those who believe that the professor has no business with anything except transmitting factual and technological knowledge. For example, they believe that a professor giving a course in theories and forms of government should not try to influence the student in favor of one or the other; the professor is a scientist and is concerned with the analysis of facts only. The choice between alternatives is up to the student. If he has done a good job of analysis, the student will have been prepared to draw his own value conclusions. As Robert Frost puts it in the *Cabin in the Clearing* these professors

> . . . . live in the faith accumulated fact
> Will of itself take fire and light the world up.
> Learning has been part of their religion.

Whatever moral education is necessary is the responsibility of the home, the school, the church, and society. The business of higher education is to educate, not to indoctrinate. The professor is a teacher, not a preacher. Those who are of this opinion sometimes add in justification of their position that it would in any case be a waste of time to try to influence students' convictions, since these have already been formed by the time the student comes to college. Finally, they argue, what right has an instructor to try to influence the student to accept the instructor's scale of values? Although they do not really belong to this class, let us mention here a very special, and numerically rather limited class of professors who believe that it is their sole function to educate future professors, who in turn will educate their students to be professors, and so on until the end of time. As someone has said, they resemble Ubangi witch doctors who transmit their secrets only to their successors and thus keep them within the profession.

At the other extreme from those who believe in what we might call complete moral neutrality are the professors who feel it to be part of their professional obligation to direct the student in his choice of moral values. Sometimes they go so far as to indoctrinate them with their own convictions. If the student has beforehand committed himself to the "wrong" ones, or to the wrong means for promoting the "right" ones, it is the responsibility of the professor to convert him to the right values.

Between these two extreme positions lie a number of positions which represent degrees of mixtures of both. Some professors of the indoctrination persuasion feel that they should exercise such persuasion only during periods of serious domestic or foreign crisis, say during an election or during a war.

The third variable which helps to determine the proximate character, and thus possible consequences of education, is the student. No one needs to be told that the moral consequences, as well as other kinds, are to a considerable degree determined by the intelligence, the moral personality, the interest and motivation, and the social background of the student. The professor proposes; the student disposes.

Of course, the environing society may exert a great influence, negative or positive, in determining the effects of formal education, sometimes by its mere existence, sometimes by means of specific pressures. The attitude of society towards education may vary from indifference to what is taught, e.g., in the case of such a subject as mathematics, to chronic sensitivity in the case of courses in religion or political science. Such sensitivity at times becomes acute, approaching the hysterical in times of crisis. Social attitudes not only exert influence on the students but also, at least sometimes, on the educational practices of the professor.

These facts about education once again point to the need for careful analysis of the psychology of motivation, insofar as they affect the reaction of students to formal education. By what and how are students influenced in their choice of values? In spite of the diligent study of this problem by our colleagues in psychology, and insofar as social groups are concerned, by sociology, there is much that we do not know. But there is also much that we ignore.

Little more has been done than to call attention to problems. In fact, what I have really done is to give you a report of my many years of wandering about in the mazes of our academic curriculum, of long and sometimes confused discussions in faculty and committee meetings and at regional and national professional conferences. In spite of all the education to which I have been submitted, I have not been able to reach any very definite final conclusions. My only final conclusion is one of broad policy, and it could hardly be broader, namely, that in view of the inherent complexity of the problems, the number of variables involved, the variety of solutions offered, each with much to be said for it, it might be wise not to commit ourselves to any single theory or practice, but rather to take a friendly attitude to all such points of view as are themselves moderate and tolerant of others.

There are two good reasons for this conclusion. First is the fact of the inherent and inescapable character of higher education, possibly of all formal education. Formal education in this country can be compared to what in medicine is called a "shotgun prescription." Such a prescription is used when the physician is fairly certain of the condition he wishes to correct, but not certain of exactly how this is to be done. In consequence, he aims a kind of scatterload of potential cures at the illness, hoping that one or more of them will produce the desired result. Obviously, this method would not be followed if the physician knew of a single, certain cure. In education we are faced with a similar situation and must be willing to follow the same technique.

The second reason for following this policy arises from the nature of democracy. Where there is room for so many different points of view in respect to the values which should be realized by government and other social institutions, there is certainly room in formal education for different educational theories and practices which are concerned with the identification of these values, of the facts on which they rest, and of the methods which can be used in trying to realize them. In such a society as ours there is strength in variety quite as much as there is in unity, for, as the old saying has it, our goal is unity in variety.

Luther H. Hodges

What Kind of America?

THE University of Alabama, so strategically situated in these days, is to be congratulated for its efforts to stimulate more searching discussion of what the future holds for Alabama and her sister states. We are also grateful to the other colleges and universities of the United States for their cooperation and assistance in this meeting. We need to look ahead as far and as clearly as we can. These are times of very rapid and complex change. We are all plunging headlong into a new world, whose form we are only beginning to apprehend. In too many cases we have failed to face the changed reality, to understand it, and constructively to come to terms with it.

The political, social, and economic aspects of this change in the world are all crucial for the future of the Deep South. But I have not sought to limit myself to any one of these categories. In the first place, I find it very difficult to separate these aspects of how people live and move forward together. And, secondly, I would suggest humbly and sincerely that the Deep South is not going anywhere, if it proposes to go alone. And the same can be said of any other region of this great country, or of any other country on this troubled earth of ours.

There is not much that can be said about the political future of a region or a nation these days without taking into consideration its economic and social developments. No area or society can realize its full economic potential without undergoing some significant changes in its political attitudes and its social patterns. And the failure to deal constructively with explosive social forces can wreck the best laid plans of politicians, economists, businessmen, and laboring men.

These changes and potential changes are interdependent. We can try to separate them, try to triangulate human existence in an effort to understand ourselves and our society better, but we cannot escape the fact that life is not lived, or work done, or history made in tight little compartments. Nor can we compartmentalize our lives or our thoughts or our southern society. If we try to make progress in one area and try to cling to that part of the past that is outmoded, we will inevitably fail in both. And if we try to talk and think about the South as if it had some mystical and independent destiny, our talk and thought will be irrelevant to the future.

Not many people today seriously are chanting "save your Confederate money, boys, the South will rise again." But there is a more sophisticated appeal to southern pride and sentiment which suggests that the South, in coming into its own economically, is going to forge ahead of the rest of the nation, and thus will avenge the wrongs done to it in the past by inheriting the nation, if not the earth, economically. Today, we rejoice in the progress the whole South has made in the last two or three decades. There has been a virtual revolution in southern agriculture since the end of World War II, as well as a rapid growth of its industry. Along the Gulf Coast there has grown up a magnificent petrochemical complex. On the Savannah River there is a $2 billion nuclear production facility, as well as nuclear research facilities on southern university campuses. The South is a leader in the utilization of educational television. And here in Alabama, at Huntsville, as well as Cape Kennedy in Florida, and at other southern locations, the South stands on the threshold of the space age.

But, as a governor of a southern state, I was constantly aware of the larger context in which I had to work—a context ranging far beyond the South and even the United States. For example, I was concerned long before it became a headline matter with the United States' balance of payments deficit and the drain on our nation's gold reserves. This was having a very indirect, but nevertheless very powerful impact upon our efforts to create more jobs in North Carolina.

What was happening? Our country—our businessmen, our tourists, and our government—was spending more in other countries than foreign countries were spending with us. Dollars were accumulating in the hands of these foreign holders at an alarming rate, and there was a growing tendency for them to convert their dollars into gold from our reserves. They were afraid we would be forced to devalue the dollar—reduce its value in terms of gold—to prevent the exhaustion of our reserves, and also to reduce the prices of American exports, so we could sell more abroad and thereby earn more to offset our overseas expenditures. But the dollar is the keystone of the international monetary system and of our whole system of international trade. It is accepted by buyers and sellers the world over because it is "as good as gold." So devaluation of the dollar, and the destruction of this trading system built up again after World War II, was unthinkable. And it probably would have been ineffective because other countries would have devalued too, to maintain the same rates of exchange.

All of this meant that the United States had to keep its interest rates high to prevent even more money from flowing abroad—attracted by the prospects of earning more in foreign banks that pay even higher rates of interest. But higher interest rates at home tend to discourage businessmen from borrowing money to invest in new plants which would create more jobs. It also encouraged corporations with surplus cash to put it into savings accounts rather than use it to expand or modernize their facilities. And when fewer new plants are being built and fewer older plants expanded, North Carolina and Alabama and every other state has a much harder time of attracting or creating new industrial jobs for its workers, who have been leaving our farms at a rapid pace and looking for jobs in the towns and cities. Fortunately, the run on our gold reserves has been reduced to a trickle. This Administration convinced foreign dollar holders that we would not devalue our currency. We have also worked out some special arrangements with foreign governments and their central banks to safeguard the dollar from future speculation. But we still have a serious deficit problem, and it concerns the Deep South as much as it does the New York bankers who handle the bulk of our international gold and currency transactions.

It is important to you that our national export expansion program, sponsored by the United States Department of Commerce, should succeed. Your prospects for future economic growth will be affected by the vigor with which businessmen in other parts of the country enter and succeed in the foreign market, just as their growth will be affected by how Deep South businessmen accept the challenge to sell more abroad.

It is important to your future that we modernize our industrial plants throughout the United States. Much of our equipment is older than the machines put in place, with much United States' aid, since World War II in Western Europe and Japan. This lack of modernization impairs our productivity. We are not producing goods as cheaply as we could to win more sales in other countries and to meet the competition of foreign goods in American markets. It is also important to your future that we do a better job of applying scientific research to our civilian production, to creating new growth products and new industrial processes, and that we develop more of our potential scientific and technical brainpower, so we will have enough of these trained people for our civilian economy, as well as for our space and defense efforts. Right now the Japanese are applying as much scientific and engineering brainpower to civilian products as we are, on a per capita basis, and the West Germans are applying more.

It is important to your future that we have an expanding national economy, and that this growth take place with relative price stability. Business, labor and government must work together to stimulate our growth rate, so we will create the additional jobs we need, without the kind of inflation that could impair our domestic living standards and price American goods out of world markets.

Most important to your future is the realization that most of our problems are not North Carolina problems, or Alabama problems, or southern problems, or even in many cases American problems. Our big concerns are the problems of free men everywhere, the problems of how to achieve greater prosperity, more individual dignity and freedom, and a securer peace for all men, whatever their race, their creed, their nationality, or their present situation in life. There can be no future for the Deep South, or for the South as a whole, as a separate entity, as something apart from, fearful of, or indifferent to, the powerful forces shaping the future of our nation and the world. The world's problems are the South's problems, and the problems that face the people of the southern states are very properly the concern of people everywhere. Many people outside the South are finding that what they thought were problems peculiar to the South are explosive problems in their own communities. I regret that any community has these problems. Nevertheless, the realization of these problems represents progress in understanding the scope of the racial problem in America and in the world. Indeed, this understanding is necessary to the achievement of meaningful equality of opportunity for all people.

The rest of the nation is far less different from the South than it has imagined, and this has come as something of a shock to them. And the South has not yet fully realized how like the rest of the country it has become. Both sides need to adjust their thinking. The recent past makes it very clear that the future of the South lies in becoming more and more like the rest of the nation, and the really meaningful question is: What is our nation to become?

Despite the growth of southern cities and our industry, we still tend to think of the South as being much more agricultural than the rest of the nation. But there has been a real revolution in southern agriculture since 1940. In that year, 34 per cent of all employment in the South was in farm jobs. In the nation as a whole, farm jobs accounted for only 19 per cent of total employment. But in 1960, farm employment in the South had plunged to only 9 per cent of total employment—while dropping to 7 per cent in the United States as a whole. The South is now only a percentage point or two away from being just like the rest of the nation in the farm/nonfarm divisions of its labor force. Farm mechanization and the creation of many new jobs in industry and the service occupations have been transforming southern life. Far from being a land of sharecroppers, the South is now essentially a land of farming by machines and chemicals. The index of mechanization in the South is now equal to that for the nation as a whole.

There are wide variations among the states and within them. North Carolina has more small farms than any other southern state, despite the fact that it also has a great deal of industry—adding more value by manufacturing than Connecticut and ranking eleventh among the 50 states in manufacturing. But the fact remains that 90 per cent of all southern families are nonfarm families. Here in Alabama, 88 per cent of your families are off the farm, for all practical economic purposes, even though many of them still may be living on the land.

The South also closely resembles the rest of the nation in its nonfarm occupational mix. In 1960, the percentage distribution of employed persons in various occupations in the South was about what it was in the rest of the nation ten years earlier. In 1964 the South is probably even closer to the national employment pattern. The big growth in job opportunities in the United States in the decade of the 1950's was not in factory jobs. It was in service and professional and technical jobs. And the South has been following that national trend. While the South had an increase of 23 per cent in craftsmen, foremen, and kindred workers, and a 19 per cent increase in factory operatives in the decade, its service workers increased 36 per cent, clerical workers 50 per cent, and professional and technical workers 52 per cent. White-collar occupations have absorbed more of our work force since 1956 than blue-collar jobs. And the number of workers in our country's service industries has exceeded the number in goods-producing industries since 1949. The shift has been toward jobs that require more and better education, and education is the key to raising the productivity and per capita income of the South.

In 1932, southern per capita income was only 53 per cent of the national figure. Twenty years later, after World War II and the growth of the early postwar period, it was 73 per cent of the national figure. The most recent figure, for 1962, is 76 per cent, or more than three-fourths of the national level.

But whether the gap closes further or even slips backwards in the next decade depends largely upon the kind of educational effort the South makes. The rest of the country is also moving ahead, and as the Red Queen explained to Alice in *Through the Looking Glass:* "It takes all the running you can do to keep in the same place. If you want to get somewhere else, you must run at least twice as fast as that."

It was estimated some time back that, if the South continued to support its educational system at the level of the 1950's—which because of increased enrollments would require a doubling of school expenditures—the region would find in 1975 that it had been slipping, not gaining on the national standard of living. It would drop from 76 per cent of the national per capita income to only 67 per cent. If, on the other hand, the South raised its level of educational support to the national average, it was projected that southern per capita income would rise to 84 per cent of the national figure in 1975, and would be almost double what it was in 1960. Southern personal income would be almost tripled, and the southern market in 1975 would be, by itself, more than half as large as the entire United States market in 1960.

As the South meets its challenges, it will become more and more like the rest of the United States and can make a great contribution to the nation. It will still be different from the United States as New England is different from the United States as a whole, or as the Midwest and the Pacific Northwest have a flavor all their own. But essentially the destiny of the South is to become what America becomes, and hopefully our contribution from the South will make for a better America. The South, in the larger sense, will be what America will be, and southerners can really only affect the destiny of their region by acting as Americans to help shape the character and destiny of their country in a rapidly changing world.

What kind of America is this going to be?

Is this going to be an America in which all of our fellow citizens, without regard to race, color, or creed, have a decent standard of living?

Is this going to be an America which has found ways of living in relative peace and harmony with other countries, including those that have radically different cultures and social systems? Will we be humble and generous in our attitudes and actions?

Is this going to be an America that is at peace within itself?

Is this going to be an America that believes in brotherhood and the American dream of freedom and equality of opportunity for all?

Is this going to be an America that refuses to be torn apart by hatred and violence, because it is capable of recognizing legitimate grievances and of moving to rectify those things which are wrong and long overdue for righting?

These are some of the really challenging questions that have to be answered in Alabama, in North Carolina, in New York and Wisconsin, and Maryland and California, if we are to have a destiny worthy of American traditions. These are the kinds of problems that knock insistently at our door—at all of our doors, whether you are students, or professors, or businessmen, or housewives, or public officials—knocking and demanding the best that is in us, demanding that we accept the call to leadership, that we make the nation's crucial human problems our individual, personal concerns.

This America of ours is the richest society ever known to man. Last year our gross national product topped $600 billion, and the take-home-pay of Americans totaled more than $400 billion, after taxes. Yet there are about 35 million Americans—one-fifth of our total population—who shared, not one-fifth or even one-tenth of that vast sum. Their share was less than one-twentieth of the disposable personal income of the United States. Only $11 billion a year would raise all of these families, including more than 11 million children, out of the poverty category as it is currently defined in the United States. If a dole would solve the basic problems of these people, we could wipe out poverty in America almost overnight. But a dole is not what these people need. They need something much more difficult to mobilize. They need an aroused America, a country determined to attack the root causes of poverty, a people willing to give of their ingenuity, their concern, and their means, in their own communities, to help us make a successful final assault on poverty in America. It means that you and I, all over the nation, should not just ride from a lovely home in a modern car to a modern office, but should look around our towns and cities to see how our fellow citizens are living.

In our city slums, in our rural shacks, in the camps of migrant workers, on our Indian reservations, around long-closed mine shafts, there is real privation, frustration, and degradation. There is disease and delinquency and crime. There is poverty that is real, painful, and seemingly hopeless and self-perpetuating—and intensely personal! We need to find ways in our local communities, in our states, and through our national government, to break this tragic chain of ignorance, apathy, and want. We need to discover ways of making better use of our existing welfare and economic development programs, including the community development programs of the Commerce Department's vital Area Redevelopment Administration. We need to develop new and bolder approaches to some of these ancient problems—such as the regional approach of the Appalachia Commission, which seeks to revitalize an area of some 16 million people extending from northern Alabama to the Pennsylvania coal fields.

We can stop wringing our hands over the large number of our young men who fail the pre-induction examinations given by the armed services under the Selective Service program. We can, instead, try to equip these young men for productive work, through the Job Corps program recommended to the Congress by President Johnson. We can give them better educations, and we must. An astonishing one-third of all our southern young men examined under the Selective Service program from 1950 through 1962 failed to pass the mental qualification test. In North Carolina it was 34.5 per cent. In Alabama it was more than 40 per cent, and in Mississippi it was 45 per cent—or four times the 11.5 per cent figure for the rest of the nation. Should we not in the South ask ourselves the question—why such a difference?

These figures reflect, not upon the inherent ability of our people, but upon the lack of education or the quality of the education we have been giving our youth. We must realize that, in addition to trying to correct the deficiencies of the past, we are challenged to raise the level of support for our schools at every level. And we must challenge our schools at all levels to do a better job of training. Our citizens must demand better leadership and support this leadership to the limit. We must make even greater sacrifices for the future, if we are not to saddle our country and our region with large numbers of men and women who, because of inadequate educations today, will be of little value to our economy, or themselves, in tomorrow's even more complex, highly technical society.

Our ability to make some of the greater expenditures needed to realize the full potential of the South in a growing America will depend upon what happens in our relations with other countries, and especially with the Soviet bloc countries. There has been a marked turn for the better in our relations with the Soviet Union, an improvement stemming from a mutual understanding that each side has the power and the determination to defend its vital national interests, but that neither country wants to unleash a nuclear holocaust. No one knows what the future may hold for our relations with the Soviet Union or with its various allies and satellite states. But whether we can develop slowly more normal relations with these countries, through limited agreements or through expanding trade in non-strategic goods, it is as important to the future of the South as anything that might happen in Dixie itself.

We can safely and logically expand our non-strategic trade with the Soviet bloc countries in Europe. Most of these goods are already available to these countries from other Western industrial nations. In 1962, all of the countries of the free world sold nearly $4.5 billion worth of goods to the Soviet bloc in Europe. And of these sales, about half—$2.2 billion—were shipments from Japan and our North Atlantic Treaty Organization allies. United States sales totaled only $125 million, and these were largely agricultural commodities. With so many sources of supply for modern industrial goods, one country such as the United States cannot prevent the Soviet Union from obtaining the things it needs to develop its economy. We have to be realistic in the application of our export controls, and our people must be sophisticated enough to recognize opportunities to serve our national interest by expanding trade as well as by restricting it.

There is, of course, no challenge facing America which demands greater realism than the explosive problem of equal opportunity for all our citizens, regardless of race, creed, or color. This is a problem which could tear America apart. It could destroy all hopes for developing the potential of the South, all efforts to maintain the United States as a bulwark of freedom and democratic self-government, and all dreams of building a world in which no man's hand is raised in anger against his brother. It could plunge this great country of ours into an orgy of hatred and violence in which today's militants on both sides would be devoured by more extreme leadership tomorrow, and tomorrow's extremists by even more radical leaders the day after. We are witnessing a social revolution centering on the demands of Negro rights, and given the whole history of this nation and of the world itself, the ultimate outcome cannot be in doubt. The Negro in America cannot be forever denied equal opportunity and the full measure of human dignity without the abandonment of everything America has stood for in the history of Western civilization. The Negro deserves better treatment, and he must surely get it.

Our good sense will not permit us to continue to sanction the waste of the talents of our Negro citizens. We are educating all of our citizens at great expense, and then allowing a large number of these trained people to be used in jobs far below their potential. Far too many trained Negro engineers are still sweeping floors, sorting mail, and digging ditches. Trained stenographers are working as maids. Trained electricians are raking leaves, and men trained as draftsmen can find jobs only as construction laborers. Significantly, one of the reasons for our low per capita income in the South is the widespread underemployment of Negroes in our labor force. Less than half of our Negro families are headed by persons with full-time, year-round jobs. Too many Negro men and women are confined to jobs that produce little for them or for those who employ them—to jobs which in other parts of the country have been partially eliminated by machines, with a resulting rise in the average productivity and average incomes of the people in those areas.

The South can never realize its full potential as long as a substantial portion of its population is functioning far below its capacity. We cannot maintain the employment traditions of a plantation economy and expect to be a leader or even a full participant in a highly technical national and international economy. But even if the South or the nation could afford this waste, it would not be possible to maintain in an open, democratic society practices and traditions which an overwhelming majority of the people know in their hearts to be unfair, intolerable, and morally wrong. This is the reality we must face, if we are to make the difficult adjustments and accommodations that are necessary to prevent a rending of our social fabric by extremists on both sides.

There are those, white and Negro, who would rather see America pulled apart than have it wear a cloth that is not cut according to their own measurements. But these extremists cannot prevail in a nation, in a state, or in a community, whose citizens are willing to speak for what is right and to work for what is good. They cannot prevail if enough Americans are willing to accept a full share of the responsibility for determining what America is to become.

Let it be said clearly again and again. We must all respect the law and obey the law. Change it if we will, but obey it until and unless it is changed. And this message is to white and Negro alike, of whatever shades of color and whatever shades of opinion. It is also to bad politicians (most politicians are good, honest leaders)—to those politicians who incite and encourage trouble to garner votes for themselves. This sort of politician should be rebuked and refused support. Most of us throughout this great nation—the South, the West, the East, and North—are moderate in our thinking and in our actions. Let's be unafraid as we face today's problems. Let's be courageous and firm in our support of what is right. It is up to each of us to help decide what America is to become.

We can help history decide whether America had the power to bring out the best in her citizens, whether it could inspire them with compassion for the unfortunate, whether it could sustain their faith in the future in a revolutionary world, whether it could give them a permanent passion for justice and truth and the achievement of the brotherhood of man. America's challenges are our challenges, and America's hope for the future lies in our response to them.

THE DEEP SOUTH IN TRANSFORMATION

Training for Responsible Citizenship

Oliver C. Carmichael

The Social Sciences and Training for Responsible Citizenship

THE SOCIAL SCIENCES, the humanities, and natural sciences constitute the three divisions of basic knowledge. One of the functions of each of these is the orientation of youth to its world, providing some understanding of the hopes, aspirations, and requirements of its society. A brief discussion of each of these divisions should help to identify more clearly the role of the social sciences in university training.

The dictionary definition of the humanities is "the branches of learning concerned with human thought and relations as distinguished from the sciences." This description of the nature and scope of the humanities suggests an acquaintance with one's culture, heritage, and background. Through the Greek and Roman classics, literature, philosophy, and history the student begins to understand something of the foundations of his society. Through the humanities young people become oriented with respect to their past. They are given a bird's-eye view of important developments in the area of "thought and relations," its ideals as expressed in great literature, its struggles to achieve them, as recorded in history, and its conclusions as summed up in its philosophy.

In contrast with the humanities, the social sciences are concerned with the present social organization, the nature and variety of social institutions, the currents and countercurrents operative among them, our sociological, economic and political system, its social history and philosophy, its economic history and philosophy, and its political history and philosophy. Just as the humanities seek to orient youth with respect to their past, so the social sciences are concerned with the orientation of youth with respect to the present complex structure of society with its conflicting claims and insistent demands. Humanistic studies are prerequisite to an understanding of the social sciences; hence are freely brought into this discussion.

These studies enable young people to interpret their historic culture and to understand their heritage as the social sciences are designed to acquaint them with the motivations, the complexities, and the compulsions of modern society. Through knowledge of the past, an understanding of themselves and of the social milieu of which they are a part is acquired. In this way humanistic-social studies assist youth in adjustment to their environment as well as to the field of scholarship and learning.

The natural sciences, the third division of the curriculum, are concerned with an understanding of the world of nature. Youth must learn to adjust to the forces of nature as well as to social forces. Need of some knowledge of nature and her laws led to the study of natural philosophy which in time gave birth to the natural sciences. Thus, the natural sciences were introduced as humane subjects into the college curriculum.

Knowledge of science and technology has been the greatest challenge to human effort. Man's conquest of nature, derived from the knowledge of her laws, has affected the lives of all of us. Scientific and technological advances have resulted in vast changes in the social, economic, and political life of our society. Some knowledge of these facts is essential to effective orientation and adjustment to the modern world.

Humanists and social scientists must include it in their preparation for citizenship.

It is of equal or greater importance that science majors likewise understand the meaning of the humanities and social sciences. One of the serious current problems in some quarters is lack of interest and faith in the humanistic-social studies. The overwhelming preoccupation with science and technology, to the neglect of other subjects, is a characteristic fault of our time. The place of the social sciences and the humanities in training for responsible citizenship will be profoundly influenced by the faith which society has in the humanistic-social studies as a means of advancing the cause of social progress, for the support of these studies will depend upon the public's belief in their importance.

Within recent years a renaissance of interest in mathematics, physics, and biology has resulted from the advances made not only in the knowledge of these subjects but also in methods of instruction. For more than a century no basic changes had been made in the subject matter of these courses or in the methods of teaching them. The release of atomic energy, the expansion of knowledge in the natural sciences, and the new approaches to scientific research which were discovered during World War II resulted in a new outlook, in new fields of study, and in new methods of instruction. This has resulted in a new emphasis upon science and technology and in new methods of teaching. Calculus, formerly a junior college subject, is now being taught in some high schools.

Interest in humanistic-social studies now lags in much the same way as interest in physics and mathematics did before World War II. The revolutionary changes which have taken place in mathematics and the sciences suggest that similar reforms in content, method, and approach in the humanities and social sciences might also occur. Some new bold and imaginative attack on the problems of research and instruction in non-science subjects is long past due. A frank recognition of the differences in methods and purposes of scientific and humanistic-social studies is essential to much needed reforms in both undergraduate and graduate education.

The current advances in science and technology center around the discovery of atomic energy and the means of releasing it for human use. Atomic fission opened up many new fields of investigation for the scientists and technologists. Changes in research and instruction have been the result and the end is not yet. New discoveries lead to new frontiers and ever-expanding knowledge. It is this which has transformed scientific instruction and research.

In the humanistic-social studies field the counterpart of the atom is, in one sense, the idea. Ideas like atoms have hidden powers as our century has amply demonstrated. Fascism, naziism, and communism have arisen in our time and have flourished. They make it clear that ours is an ideological as well as a technological age, a fact which is sometimes forgotten, or ignored. No widespread and thorough analytical study of the ideologies of the twentieth century, which had the explosive force of crusades, has been made. Why have these concepts, to which millions of lives have been sacrificed, attracted so little scholarly attention? If some disease had ravaged the populations of the world, vast sums would have been spent and many thousands employed to determine the cause and to eradicate it, but apparently little fundamental research has been directed toward understanding the scourge of totalitarianism, in all its forms, its causes and the means of its elimination. Instead, theses and dissertations in the social sciences have often dealt with trivial topics. They rarely reflect concern over important issues of the day.

Instruction and research in the humanities and social sciences have apparently paid too little attention to the revolutionary changes occurring in our society or the changes which the future has in store for us. Foundation support for foreign area and language programs began in the 1940's, and the government has within the past decade made some grants in this field, but in the main the program of research and instruction in the colleges and the universities in the non-scientific fields has remained unchanged. In short, the humanistic-social studies program is in business as usual, giving little indication that anything of importance has happened in the past decade or two that should affect it.

When so much change has occurred in the natural sciences and so little in the humanities and social sciences in the past half century, several questions arise. Is there nothing new in our time that challenges the humanist and the social scientist? Have the humanistic-social studies been so fully developed that no change has been needed in the past fifty years? Or, has basic progress been so limited in the past few decades that there is no basis for a new approach in teaching or in research?

The building blocks of the structure of organized society are ideas, concepts, and ideals. They have evolved slowly and have been implemented even more gradually in the six thousand years of recorded history. They are imbedded in the great literature, history, art, and philosophy of the past. Each basic idea or concept has a history. The classics of all cultures in the main embody those ideas that have proved sound, constructive, and foundational. No comprehensive effort has been made to identify these basic ideas and concepts which undergird our culture.

No systematic effort has been made to identify and analyze concepts that have proved constructive or destructive, and yet such knowledge is surely basic to the understanding and development of sound human relations. Moreover, the foundations of the social sciences are the basic ideas, concepts, and ideals upon which organized society rests. The handicaps to progress are obvious when it is realized that the basic elements have never been identified. The stage of development of the social sciences would appear to correspond roughly to that of the development of chemistry before the discovery of the chemical elements.

Undergirding every culture there are basic concepts and ideals which constitute its foundations. Knowledge of these provides an understanding of the culture itself. The reason why no systematic effort has been made to identify the basic elements may be that the task is too great for individual enterprise. Like the discovery of atomic fission, this may require a massive attack, a concert of effort. Perhaps some day the social science departments in our colleges and universities may find a greater interest in this approach to learning.

The present plight of the humanistic-social studies is such that there is, in some quarters, concern over their survival. There are those who predict that the college of arts and science may be on its way out because of a declining interest in the studies which it offers. New approaches in the curriculum and in methods of instruction and research might help in reviving an interest in these subjects. It is not inconceivable that, if attention were focused upon the excavation of the ideas buried in the history, literature, philosophy, and art of our culture, a new source of interest and motivation might be discovered which would transform the humanities and social sciences into the most exciting areas for instruction and research, outrivaling science and technology in their appeal to youth.

By building the curriculum around the basic ideas and

concepts of our culture, learning progress should be greatly accelerated because the students' interests would be concentrated on essentials, not matters of peripheral interest. A knowledge of the basic ideas and concepts which motivated the events recorded by history insures a more immediate and thorough understanding of the meaning of those events. The criteria of greatness in history, literature, and art are found in the ideas and ideals with which they deal and to which they give expression.

There is not only uncertainty and dissatisfaction with respect to the curriculum in the humanistic-social studies field but disagreement and confusion with respect to methods of instruction. There are social scientists who declare their role to be a neutral one in instruction and in leadership. They agree to discuss value systems, for example, but will not express a preference for one over another since this would violate the principle of objectivity in instruction. This applies to their role as teachers and governs their performance in the classroom. To give positive leadership seems to some to be giving up a treasured principle. Fortunately such extremism is much less common than it was before World War II.

Despite the pessimism about the future of the liberal arts, the shortcomings of the present program and the forces that militate against their welfare and progress, there are encouraging signs. A general concern is expressed on every hand by laymen as well as by educators and scholars. Businessmen, lawyers, doctors and other professional groups have been among the staunchest advocates of strong liberal arts programs. This interest has expressed itself in certain concrete ways: through the establishment of a commission on the humanities by the American Council of Learned Societies, through the introduction of a bill in Congress to provide a

National Institute of Arts and the Humanities and, finally, through the establishment of the Aspen Award, announced in November 1963, to encourage humanistic studies.

The ACLS Commission was set up in January 1963. Its purpose is to investigate and report on the following: "The present state of scholarship and teaching in the humanistic disciplines; relations between humanistic scholarship and teaching at all levels from primary school to the graduate school; sources of financial support available for research in the humanities and for curriculum development in humanistic disciplines; the adequacy or inadequacy of research materials for humanistic scholarship; present and potential importance of new techniques in humanistic teaching and scholarship." Additional matters to be considered are the relations between the humanistic studies and other areas of scholarship and creativity. On the basis of findings the Commission will be expected to seek solutions to the problems encountered and to suggest how the deficiencies may be eliminated. The Council hopes to have for the humanities the counterpart of Vannevar Bush's *Science, the Endless Frontier,* which was instrumental in the establishment of the National Science Foundation.

The small amount of support for the humanistic-social studies as compared with the sums voted for scientific research seems to have disturbed members of Congress. This bore fruit in a bill (H.R. 12560) introduced by John Fogarty, Democrat of Rhode Island, calling for the setting up of a National Institute of the Arts and Humanities within the U.S. Office of Education. The bill was referred to the Committee on Education and Labor.

Two other items are worth mentioning as indications of the deep interest of the lay public in the humanistic-social studies. One was an anonymous gift to Princeton University some three years ago, of 30 million dollars in support of studies in the humanistic-social fields. The second was the Aspen Award providing the sum of 30 thousand dollars annually for that scholar who is judged to have made the most significant contribution to the humanities.

The widespread interest in the non-science subjects of the curriculum of the college and the university is an encouraging sign. It suggests that in time the humanistic-social science disciplines may receive adequate support. With more support will come more scholars and teachers in those areas and more effective attack on the problems of making non-science subjects contribute more fully to the development of youth. A new confidence in the universities, which has been evident since World War II, should add to the chances that the social sciences will be able to achieve a break-through within the next decade, giving them an opportunity for an expanding contribution to social progress.

Someone has suggested that "we are moving into a period in which society will be organized around the universities. . . ." There is no doubt that the potential of university leadership through all areas of scholarship is much greater than it was fifty years ago. But the new faith in the universities has been built upon a narrow foundation. It is the university's effectiveness in scientific and technological research which has been responsible for the development of American confidence in our institutions of higher education. The universities must show achievements in the solution of human problems before the foundations of a new public confidence will be secure.

The social sciences already play an important role in university training in citizenship, but their full potential has never been realized, partly because there has been uncertainty and confusion about their function in the curriculum and partly because instruction has lacked clarity of purpose and firmness of position when important issues were under consideration. The great reforms in university education which lie ahead will almost certainly be in the area of the humanistic-social studies. Perhaps the American Council of Learned Societies' Commission, appointed a year ago last January, will provide a blueprint for the research and planning necessary to the development of the fullest potential of the humanities and social sciences for the next decade or two.

Comments BY JAMES L. MILLER, JR.

Dr. Carmichael's statements concerning the need for a massive increase in the amount of humanistic and social science research, and his suggestion that much of it may need to be group research, clearly are significant. Social science research is important not only in its own right, but because of its inevitable effect upon social science teaching. The institution which puts students into close association with an on-going program of research brings the social sciences to life. For evidence of this I need only to cite my own experience here at the University of Alabama. I was a graduate student here just as V. O. Key, Alex Heard, and others were winding up their Alabama-based study, *Southern Politics*. Their methodology, as well as their findings, were new and significant. The atmosphere in the Department of Political Science was electrified. Students, as well as faculty, felt close to important events, and the total intellectual climate was affected.

Some specific forms of university training for responsible citizenship also merit attention, and here again is a University of Alabama example with which I happen to be familiar: The Southern Regional Training Program in Public Administration. The SRTP program is a joint venture among three universities—Alabama, Tennessee, and Kentucky. Students at the master of arts level spend three months at each university taking course work and three months working as interns in a public agency in one of the three states. The program is in its twentieth year and over 130 carefully selected students have completed it. Most of them presently are working for some type of governmental or quasi-governmental agency, the majority of which are in the South. I mention this program not in order to recite these facts about it, but to comment upon the type of curriculum it has utilized, which I think has direct relevance to several of the ideas put forth by Dr. Carmichael—the interrelatedness of the disciplines, and the need for universities to affect social relationships rather than simply observing them. The SRTP curriculum places a particular stress upon giving to students a perspective concerning public administration. Perspective has several dimensions, including a depth of understanding, a breadth of understanding, and a longitudinal dimension which relates past, present, and future in meaningful ways. The SRTP curriculum was heavy on theory, on history, and on philosophy—all of which a university is peculiarly well-suited to present—and, if the curriculum were trimmed, it was on the how-to-do-it side, which one has the opportunity to learn on-the-job.

Over the past twenty years young people have been going out of this program and into governmental positions in southern and non-southern states. Many of them now hold important state, local, and federal jobs. There is no hesitancy on my part in asserting, because I have seen specific evidence on more than one occasion, that the emphasis upon perspective in the SRTP program has enabled these people to make important contributions to the adjustments which our social organizations, including government, have been called upon to make in this rapidly changing world.

This is of particular importance in the South, because the South is changing especially fast. Indeed, the modern South has become one of the major sociological field laboratories in North America. As a place in which social change can be studied and influenced, it is rivaled on this continent only by the giant cities of the eastern and central states which also are experiencing rapid changes, but of a different kind. In the world outside North America, only the underdeveloped countries provide a comparable challenge.

A reporter for a major national news magazine the other day requested transfer from San Francisco to Atlanta, where he travels over much of the Southeast. Asked why he had requested the transfer, he looked surprised and said, "Because this is where the biggest domestic news story of our generation is going on and I want to be here to see it." None of us who live in the South is unaware of that fact, but how fully have we taken it into account as social scientists? How much have we utilized this opportunity to study at first-hand a major social revolution, with all its concomitant effects upon government and upon other forms of social organization? Some opportunities are purely fortuitous accidents. Many more are opportunities that we make for ourselves. And there also is an added extra increment of opportunities which come, rather like interest on an investment, to those who are known to have successfully taken advantage of previous opportunities. The contributions which the social sciences have made in the Deep South are due to those people who have taken their opportunities and used them well. The failures of the social sciences to make as full a contribution as they might have, or as the region might have benefited from, are due in large measure to a failure to recognize and utilize opportunities. In a region that is changing more rapidly than any other in our nation, this failure is attributable sometimes to prudence, and sometimes to fear. Prudence, when it is genuine, is an aspect of wisdom. All too often, however, prudence is a rationalization for lesser things than wisdom. Luckily, our region has been blessed with a fair number, and the number is growing, of men and women, many of them social scientists, who combine wisdom and courage.

Comments BY PHILIP G. HOFFMAN

In retrospect, each of the transitional stages of human history has experienced in different degrees the anxieties of change from the familiar to the unknown. To the living generations the past has always been inadequate; the present extremely demanding; and the future fraught with concern for the unknown. H. G. Wells, in his *Outline of History,* expressed his concept of the future in 1920 when he said: "Human history becomes more and more a race between education and catastrophe." Sputnik re-emphasized Wells's feelings about six years ago, and the space race projected itself into every home in this country. Since then Americans everywhere have found themselves propelled into a future-related-present. With the stimulation provided by space-related research, experimentation, and production, our educators are obliged to develop an academic environment for youth whose world is designed by the scientist, calculated by the computer, and structured by the engineer. Yet, these young people must develop vision, flexibility, creativity, understanding, and stability if the "space race is not to out-distance the human race." Tomorrow's youth must be capable of making judgments representative of the cumulative humanity that has produced him. He must reconcile his values with the worths transmitted through his heritage if his roots are to be secure and his continuity in the stream of human events is to be effective. Tomorrow's youth must develop the foresight to endow him with supremacy over tyranny and salvation from destruction by the mechanizations of his own creation.

This realization emphasizes the seriousness of the deficiencies in the development of the social sciences. It underscores the critical need for dramatic progress in research and vital teaching in the social sciences. To achieve this progress will require a special dedication and commitment in this and the other institutions of this great land. The tremendous advances which have occurred in the sciences, engineering, and mathematics have in large part been stimulated because they have been identified with problems of personal and national security. No less momentous questions of survival are involved in the proper development of the social sciences. The problem is how to create a climate of awareness which will make possible the dramatization of the critical need for this development.

Real progress will demand renewed dedication to the importance of the individual, a concept which exerted a vital influence in the emergence of this nation and has been responsible for much of its amazing growth and development. There are indications that the anxieties of recent years have caused us to become somewhat less concerned with the importance of the individual. I suggest this is related in a fundamental way to the problem of the failure of the social sciences to develop to potential.

Maximum progress will require devotion to the integrity of the university as well as to the individual. Such integrity will ensure at all times an atmosphere conducive to the free enterprise in ideas which is so essential to healthy development of the social sciences. A university's primary dedication must be to seek the truth and make it known. Its faculty must at all times have an abiding assurance of the support of the administration in its endeavor. It frequently happens that truth is found on the battlefield of controversy. The society which expects its universities to seek the truth must at all times be willing to allow a measure of strife if it expects them to achieve truth. Such an atmosphere is essential to the vital development of the social sciences.

Comments BY JOHN W. BLOOMER

It is my privilege to interpret my participation in this discussion of the social sciences and university training for responsible citizenship as a tribute to the institution to which I have devoted a good part of my life, the American press, and its historic contribution to the format of the American society. The press informs; at times, too, it may misinform. Inevitably, the press, too, educates, although some may give it a poor grade in this category. It persuades, and it convinces, although in some of its more flamboyant efforts to convince, such as around election time, it can experience some spectacular failures.

Whatever may be the caliber of its contribution in these areas of intellectual influence, the daily press is a textbook of the social sciences for the American masses. That is a humbling, if not a rather frightening, responsibility for an editor scrambling to put together seven or eight editions a day for a half a million readers. Nobody is more keenly aware than the editor of the inadequacies of his commercial product for the stupendous task of inspiring mass civic responsibility. He knows he cannot provide the basic education in responsible citizenship but only the reminders. In most cases his publication, by the definition of news, recounts the failures in civic responsibility rather than the successes, the breakdowns in good citizenship rather than the achievements.

Can any of us be satisfied with the level of civic responsibility as we look around us? Can we feel pleased with the solutions that are posed for our approval to problems that seem to grow knottier and knottier in the complications of our social order today? Can we always be inspired by the goals that are set before us? And if not, where must we look for the source of our dissatisfaction? Newspapers, assuredly, as the medium of mass communication, would have to accept some of the blame. But can we not look to our universities as the primary agent for creating an intelligent, responsible climate in which the most beneficial, the most historically just, the most enlightened social order can be fostered and maintained? Do we not look to the universities to provide the trail blazers in science and in technology? Do we not look to the universities to impart the traditional and inspire the original in literature and the arts? Can we not look with justification to the universities for methods and inspiration in improving and refining in their application the principles and tenets of that which we know as Western civilization? Can we not anticipate, as the products of our institutions of higher learning step off the campus and into the social order, an individual keenly aware of responsibilities for civic, as well as professional, leadership, and equipped with the knowledge and proper values for exercising it?

The course is not to be recommended, but if necessary we in Alabama could import, even from foreign countries, engineers to plan and supervise industrial and technological programs and operations. We could import, too, scientists for research, and have been doing it very successfully in some areas of our state. But good, responsible citizenship is not an importable item. We must create and maintain that within our own society.

Educating teachers who can carry a dynamic program in the social sciences to students below the university level is a mission of the institution of higher learning that is basic. Developments in the educative program in this category in my county are heartening. A cautious but solid approach to study of the two great contesting social systems of the world today is being made. Teachers are receiving training for this project through special university courses. Experimental areas in social studies are being created for three of the high schools. Our school system feels a strong responsibility for advancing the frontiers in this segment of the curriculum.

Of great importance, too, is creating the elements of enlightened citizenship among those entering the other professions. Of immediate importance to the social order are good citizen-lawyers, good citizen-engineers, good citizen-businessmen, good citizen-scientists, good citizen-agriculturalists. Enlightened as to the opportunities within society for improvements and inspired to provide leadership for realizing them, these individuals are the instruments for a more rewarding social order.

A critical concern today is the migration of many of our most promising young people to other areas. Economic opportunities without doubt are a major bait. But do we not also have cause to wonder if unsolved problems within our social order, the uncertainty, even reluctance, with which we tend to face the future are a deterrent to these people in exploiting economic opportunities awaiting them at home? Another important test for our society at this time is created by the stresses and strains of transition from a rural agricultural order to an urban society. In that, of course, we share a problem of national scope, and solutions are evidently being found no faster in other areas than our own.

The burdens of citizenship are less acute, less demanding, seemingly, for the more elemental society generated by a rural economy. And the products of that society have always been viewed with more admiration than those of our urban areas. Thomas Jefferson must have had some bitter experiences in New York and Philadelphia to have come to the conclusion that "the mobs of great cities add just so much to the support of pure government as sores do to the strength of the human body." And Cato, several centuries before that, saluted rural citizenship with the pronouncement that "the agricultural population produces the bravest men, the most valiant soldiers, and a class of citizens the least given of all to evil designs."

If the challenges of urban citizenship were crucial in Jefferson's time, they are reaching a point almost beyond comprehension today. Within the last decade or so, 400,000 Alabamians have uprooted themselves from the social securities of the rural society to join what Jefferson called "mobs" of the cities. I am not aware of any evidence that the urban society's problems are ameliorated by receiving into its midst products of the rural society. Unfortunately, it seems to be quite the reverse.

Obligations of responsible citizenship keyed to the interdependencies of urban living must be met if Jefferson's "sores" are not to become even more inflamed. Could this be the time to accept with resignation sublimation of the social sciences in our educative structure? And what of that unparalleled, almost unprecedented challenge posed for the United States in creating a harmonious, adjusted bi-racial society within the framework of our American institutions? This overshadows all else in a test of the solidity of our social structure. For 100 years our nation has side-stepped gingerly a face-to-face confrontation with this test. It can no longer be avoided. The elements, involving bitter prejudices and deep-seated emotions, are of a revolutionary, rather than evolutionary, nature. We await the outcome with the most grave concern.

Every facet of responsible citizenship will be called on if the character of our nation is to survive. Unavoidably there will be changes in the national character. The hope is that they will be comparatively minor. Many, emotionally rather than intellectually motivated, are unable to find consolation even in that. Our universities and colleges are being tested today in the cyclonic surge of these political and economic developments. The sophistication and skill with which we screen and select our leaders, the wisdom with which we decide the speed and direction of our national course depend very largely on the caliber of exports from our university and college campuses. It is from this group that we have the right to expect civic leadership in this time of crisis. On this premise am I asking too much of the university, the college? Is the obligation on the university, the college as a primary source of the responsible citizen for this nation undeserved, unrealistic? The answer is an emphatic no.

THE DEEP SOUTH IN TRANSFORMATION

Challenge to Research

Everett C. Hughes

The Sociological Point of View

WE COULD REVIEW, just as well, not the challenge of the Deep South to research in the social sciences, but rather the challenge of social research to the Deep South. Any society presents a challenge to those who would study it: the challenge to unlock its secrets, and to question its image of itself. The secrets are of two kinds, those which people hide from outsiders, and those which they hide from themselves. Human beings are adept at keeping both, and are equally adept at prying out other people's secrets. The social scientist, insofar as he becomes adept at finding out things about other people, and about societies, plays the uneasy game of the thief catching a thief. His relation with the people he studies is never comfortable. It is a toss-up whether it is easier for an insider, or for an outsider.

Every region, or society, is at any given time a sort of God-given laboratory for study of some particular problem, and in time of crisis, especially so. A situation of great tension and crisis is, however, not necessarily easy to study. This is indeed a time of crisis in the Deep South. The crisis, however, is more than regional. It is national; indeed it is world-wide. It is here the crisis that comes from the determined and widespread effort of Negroes to take possession of the rights which they consider to belong to all Americans and from the bitter-end fanatical resistance of many other Americans to their exercise of those rights. There has been equally bitter resistance to social changes in other times and places, but usually social scientists have not been there to study it, or have either not had the courage to do it, or were prevented from it by Draconian measures. It is this extreme resistance which offers the two-way challenge of social research to the Deep South, and of the Deep South to social research.

Sociologists in these, the years of their prosperity, have tended to limit themselves to the middle range, not only of theory, but of social behavior itself. In the large survey, a national sample of people are asked at their front door or inside the house a set of standard questions about some matter of general concern. Allowance is made for a variety of answers; there are "probes" to follow out unusual attitudes. Yet the mass survey, whether of political opinion or consumer preferences, loves the small differences in the great clusters at the middle of the curve. In the recent studies based on an interviewing of a national sample of the college graduating class of 1960 about their plans for further study, one finds an analysis of the characteristics of students who plan to study law; but women are excluded from the analysis because they are too small a percentage of the total. In a study of the religious practices of Catholics in a Florida town some years ago, the Spanish speaking majority was left out because they were not "typical." Negroes similarly are omitted from the sample in many market surveys. There was no Negro college included in the sample which Paul Lazarsfeld studies in the book, *The Academic Mind,* on academic freedom. People may be left out because they are few, are not typical, or because their behavior shows some extreme deviation from the expected and the respectable.

The people at the extreme ends of the scale in their opinions and people who differ basically in their social experience from the rest of a population (women from men,

Negroes from whites) confuse the findings. One can understand certain practical reasons why exceptional people and exceptional behavior are excluded from large surveys. There are, one suspects, often more subtle reasons, such as conscious or unconscious exclusion of the odd ones from the ranks of those who count socially, morally, politically, or economically. It is fair to say that the methods used by most American sociologists tend to keep them away from peculiar people and from extremes of behavior. Their mood of objectivity is also sometimes taken to mean a certain lack of concern with people of queer beliefs. It is the trend that counts. There are certain assumptions, though, underlying both the mass survey as method and the attitude that it is the mass that counts. One is the assumption of peace, of a continuation of the status quo, or of none but rather small changes from year-to-year. When there are drastic changes, great movements for social change, it usually turns out that social scientists, if they have been predicting catastrophe, have predicted the wrong one.

Since the mass destruction of European cities from the air during the last war, the searing of Hiroshima and Nagasaki, and the subsequent development of the power to destroy to unbelievable heights, certain government agencies have studied how people will behave in extreme disaster. Teams of graduate students were recruited to be ready to go at a moment's notice to scenes of accident, storm, or flood. It was difficult to get them since a disaster, being unpredictable, might occur at examination time or on a holiday. The routine of life and the demands of the academic career militate against doing research which requires that one be ready, as is a fireman, to answer a call day or night. Not the least part of the difficulty was to "pre-test" questions for unpredictable events, although that was, in fact, overcome fairly easily on the assumption that the problems of meeting major community disasters vary less than the causes of the disaster.

Whatever the failings of social scientists themselves—timidity, love of the routine and of the expected—some extremes of behavior are hard to study because the people so behaving do not easily submit themselves to observation. When one of my students wanted to study the people who call themselves Jehovah's Witnesses, he had to pose as a potential convert. The Witnesses admit no neutrality. A postulant must try to convert his own mother by giving her the hard word that she will go to hell if she does not believe. One must be an insider, one of the faithful; or one is an outsider, one of the damned. The only third position is that of postulant, undergoing instruction and passing the hard tests of initiation into the church. Objective observer is not an admissible role. The Witnesses, however, are ordinarily without influence or power in their community. They can prevent inquiry only by not letting the observer into their houses and meetings or into their confidence.

A variation on this theme is found in the study of a science-fiction sect, *When Prophecy Fails,* by Leon Festinger. The members of the sect, so few as to meet in a private house, gathered to prepare themselves for the coming of their master in a flying saucer to save the faithful few from a new deluge. The only possible way to observe the group was to join it. Festinger and several associates did so. They joined in the preaching, prophesying, and the visions. At times the observers, feigning full faith, were nearly as numerous as those whom the observers believed sincere members. It was a small, tense group in which the role of objective observer on the sidelines would have been impossible. Although some students of mine took part in the study, I did not like the pretense involved, partly on principle and partly because of the possibility that great harm might be done.

Thus, on the bias, we approach the question of sociological research in the Deep South, asking in what role it can be done on the problem that is the most crucial one. There are many people in the South who allow no free discussion of the relations of people of European descent with the American Negro. Some have resorted to extreme forms of behavior to prevent such discussion and any deviation from practice. Some would defend their beliefs and the current practices to the death, the death certainly of others and probably of themselves. It is a case in which people feel and act upon the notion that he who is not fully with us is against us. Part of the challenge, taken in either direction, then is that of studying last-ditch defense, for people engaged in it are not likely to allow themselves to be studied fully and freely.

One of the problems in such a case is that unanimity of attitudes may not be so great as the unanimity of outward expression. Indeed, studies made by the survey method show marked changes in racial attitudes on the part of many people. Insofar as the survey method uses the private interview, and insofar as the people interviewed trust the interviewer's promise not to reveal identities, the survey may be, contrary to what I suggested, the best way to study situations of tension. But it does not study the aspect of things we are most interested in, namely, the circumstances in which those who may in privacy express a contrary opinion will state that contrary opinion in the political and social discourse of the home town. Indeed, we might ask in what circumstances people will state their contrary opinion with the same force as the extreme defenders of the publicly prevailing extremist opinion. A few people do so in the Deep South, perhaps more do so in South Africa. In either case, if they are white people, they may have a very difficult time. I know a professor whose telephone has been tapped, whose wife and daughters are given obscene scoldings over the phone at all hours of day and night because of exercising a freedom of expression and action that would have been considered normal in universities throughout the world throughout most of the history of the university as an institution. He is not alone. A young man who teaches in a private white college has related that he has moved within a block of the campus because life has become unpleasant for his wife and children. In both cases, the attacks came from outside the academic community, but they came. There is evidence that in a Virginia community, where last-ditch defense took the form of closing the public schools, the traditional leaders of more moderate views gave way, without a struggle, to people of extreme views who in normal times would not aspire to positions of leadership and would not be considered for them. It may be that last-ditch defense of this kind brings about a shifting of leadership away from the moderates. It would be good to know in what circumstances and by what means that shift could be prevented, or its direction reversed.

Some of the mechanisms involved in last-ditch defense seem to be of a universal character; others may be peculiar to American culture. A probably universal one is that of being hoisted on one's own rhetoric. To be elected to office a man declares that he will resist racial change to the death; thus he has made compromise, the essence of politics, impossible. If he retreats, he will be destroyed, politically and perhaps in other ways by the extremists whose cause he has espoused. Fanatical defenders are not unlike the political sects such as the nineteenth century anarchists in Europe in this regard; defectors were sometimes erased. Here is the phenomenon of people having talked themselves beyond the point of no return.

A more American mechanism is one adopted by the vigilantes in early and frontier days, that of not allowing the person of deviating opinion or action to remain in town. It has been used in most parts of the country at one time or another, against revenue agents, labor leaders, people of queer religion, and nowadays against peacemarchers and integrationists. What once was a defense of the vigilantes has now become a device of police, as well as of elements of the populace. Although common in the Deep South, it is by no means confined to any one region of this our country. It makes the way of the social researcher difficult, and certainly limits his ability to probe whatever differences may lie behind the wall of apparent unanimity.

If there is one thing we should have learned about modern complex societies, it is that surface unanimity is always suspect. Hitler managed to get votes of 98 per cent to 99 per cent in his favor in every election when he was in power. The question that he raised was always the same: Are you for me or against me? Unanimity on a great public issue usually is obtained only by what amount to totalitarian methods. Behind the façade of unanimous assent may hide many nuances of feeling and conscience. The presence of fanatics who have power always leads to distortion of public expression and, indeed, of private action if not of thought. One problem for social research is to find out what lies behind the façade of unanimity, and to learn how the hidden contrary opinions might be brought to expression and action.

Perhaps the most extreme of all forms of social behavior is physical violence, either in limited degree to control behavior or gain power, or to destroy other human beings. Once a popular legal form of punishment, it has lost favor in the western world both in the family, in the disciplining of children, and by public authority. In Great Britain it is part of the approved armory for educating small and middle-sized boys. It is also used in some places as punishment of incorrigible prisoners convicted of felonies. In this country the law, in the abstract, tends to disapprove much use of corporal punishment. But unofficial use, sometimes furtive, sometimes open, is probably much greater in this country than official and unofficial combined in British countries. Beating, roughing up, shocking with electrical wands, are practices used to make people move on, get out of town, or disperse. In many places in our country the police shine bright lights in the eyes of people for hours on end, weaken them with fatigue, or make them miserable in other ways either as punishment or as a form of brainwashing. If they do not have official permission to use these forms of behavior, there is at least no effective effort to make them stop. The public gives an implicit mandate to the police to conduct themselves as they do. It is no secret that these extremes are used to control Negroes more often than whites in those parts of the country, South or North, where there are Negroes in any considerable number, to control alleged "vagrants" in certain regions where migrant labor is wanted only in season, and to deal with people accused of crimes, if they are not members of some protecting group.

An opposite extreme form of behavior is non-violence, or passive resistance. In this country, violence is used by the representatives of the law as well as by many who have no mandate to punish or control others. Non-violence, with its partner passive resistance, as a rule is used by those who claim that the representatives of the law are themselves breaking the law. They maintain that legitimate authority is acting beyond or contrary to its true mandate. In India, passive resistance was eventually successful because the British-led police were loathe to use the butts of their guns on inert bodies. It has not been successful in South Africa because the police continue shooting and using their clubs. The limit of what their stomachs can stand has not been reached. The encounter of passive resistance with violence is not one of the more pleasant of human encounters, but it is one which occurs. Since it does occur, it is the business of the social scientist to observe and learn its dynamics. It is an encounter in which the role of neutral bystander (observer) is most difficult to bear as well as one in which that role is not likely to be tolerated.

There is no intent to belittle sociological research done in the South. Some of the best research done in this country has been done in the South, some of it in the Deep South. There comes to mind the many studies of regional life and culture initiated by the late Howard Odum at the University of North Carolina and carried on by his successors. Fisk University and the Tuskegee Institute have carried out many important studies on the economy and the social life and problems of the rural South. Robert E. Park and William I. Thomas, fathers of sociological research on racial and ethnic problems, held their first discussions on the dusty roads around Tuskegee just over fifty years ago. Much good work is being done now.

In the main those earlier studies had to do with problems that were real at the time. The South was rural. Its agriculture, at least the agriculture that gave the region its character, was plantation agriculture, more akin to that of the West Indies and Northern Brazil than to that of Illinois and Wisconsin, with the rotation of crops on family farms, or that of the grain-producing prairies and the ranches of the great plains. Good sociological work was done on the plantation as an institution. Those are not the problems of today. The South is becoming urban and industrial; regionalism is not a concept of much use in analyzing industrial and urban societies.

The people who worked on those plantations, where, Negro or white, literacy helped them little, are now going to the cities of the South and of the North. They are making the move not with great hope, but out of necessity. And they are making it at a time in industrial history when the demand for unlettered, unskilled labor has dwindled to naught. The result is still another kind of extreme behavior, the extreme alienation of the new urban masses, mainly from the South. They came too late, mainly because they were detained too long in the doomed plantation agriculture. It is the same whether they are Negro or white. Go into those Chicago neighborhoods invaded by rural white people from the South, and you will hear exactly the same descriptions of their behavior as of the behavior of Negroes of the same social class. They are fewer, and they are not confined behind a wall of caste, but their situation is tragic.

Those white people are, in some sense, symbolic of the present last-ditch resistance to allowing Negroes their full rights as citizens. For those unlettered whites gained nothing more than a purely symbolic victory from their position in the dominant group. They had none of the instruments of domination except their race. Whatever mutual satisfactions there may have been in the system of race relations in some places and times did not reach those people, and, indeed, have not those satisfactions pretty well disappeared throughout the South? They certainly do not exist and probably never did for most of the people who fanatically resist basic changes in the racial system. That may, indeed, lie behind their resistance; they are engaged in what Joseph Gusfield calls a symbolic crusade, when writing of the crusade against drink carried on by the people who profited least and suffered least from the evils of alcohol.

Study of the last-ditch defenders would lead one into basic changes in the social and economic structure of the South. The best of the South's social research was done on a system and social structure which no longer exist. The men who did it were good sociologists, studying what they considered the problems of their day. Even they, however, did not study the extreme behavior of the time. The study of lynching was done in the main by Negro organizations; they used for that purpose for many years, the late Walter White, a white man physiologically, who was a Negro by American definition. He could visit the site of a lynching and find out what had happened with, of course, a certain danger to his person.

One must also say that some sociologists have made it their special mission to study what happens in racial crises in the South. Thomas Pettigrew of Harvard University led a research team in Little Rock, and has continued to be as nearly Johnny-on-the-spot as possible in a number of crises, when the more extreme forms of behavior are in evidence. Others are following his lead.

Perhaps, the time will soon come when many more join the effort of observing and analyzing these extreme forms of behavior so characteristic of our country, and, in this epoch, especially of the Deep South. It is the role of the sociologists to find and observe not merely those social situations which tell us new and hitherto unknown things about human behavior, but those which are the key situations which must be described fully in objective terms if we are to understand and solve the problems of our own country in our own time. It is a task which requires great courage and great ingenuity. It is not a task for the social scientists of any one region, but for those of all regions of our country.

The challenge of the Deep South to social research is the challenge to bring in an epoch when any American can move to any part of his country and carry on his normal activities, including social research, provided they are done fairly and courageously. The general message of my words is that we are all in this together—social scientists or not, Negro or white, northerners, southerners, westerners. The Deep South like the rest of the country is going through a technological revolution which has made it urban and industrial, and will make it more so with each passing year. The challenge of the Deep South and to the Deep South is quick adaption of our institutions to this new situation with as little human destruction as possible.

Donald S. Strong

The Political Science Point of View

THE somewhat ponderous title, "The Deep South in Transformation: Challenge to Research," suggests that so far as social scientists are concerned there is something unique about the Deep South. There is. Long outside the mainstream of American life, the Deep South is distinct, both socially and politically. The conflict between the effort to launch the Deep South into the mainstream of American life and the effort to keep it in its provincial eddy produces crises and drama. No social scientist can assert that life in the South is dull. Our problem is that we are better supplied with problems worthy of research than with research money.

The researcher in a Deep South institution encounters obstacles yet possesses assets. The very word "challenge" suggests that there are obstacles to be overcome. Let us direct our attention, first, to these obstacles and then examine the assets we can utilize to meet the challenge. Incidentally, these remarks apply to this particular Deep South institution, the University of Alabama, although some of them are equally true of our sister schools.

Although the most serious long-run handicap may be that of recruiting truly able faculty in the future, there are several obstacles to those of us already on the faculty. The nearly universal twelve-hour teaching week is a major obstacle to research. While on rare occasions work load can be reduced for those directing dissertations, the beneficiaries of this relief are painfully few. Let it be said forthrightly that research and teaching conflict. The more time that must be devoted to teaching, the less time will be available for research. Skeptics may refer to some venerable figure who taught twelve hours a week all his life yet managed to publish a book every two years during his forty-five-year career. This is a little like recalling the star halfback who made Phi Beta Kappa. Both types do exist but not to a statistically significant degree. Any twelve-hour-per-week teacher who devotes much time to research talks from cold lecture notes. An extreme instance involves an acquaintance who, while teaching comparative government in 1936, confined his discussion of German government to a description of the Weimar Republic. He made no reference to the Nazi dictatorship which, having destroyed the Weimar Republic three years earlier, was to become the most important development in comparative government in this teacher's lifetime. This colleague had devoted most of his time to research in his field of special interest, which was far removed from comparative government. In his narrow area of specialization this friend is now regarded as a man of considerable stature. His example carries to the extreme the problem that every university teacher encounters. When he teaches elementary classes, he must be a generalist who needs to read broadly to keep up with a rapidly moving field. If he tries to devote much time to his own research, he may well talk from lecture notes that were thoroughly up-to-date six or seven years ago.

One would be imprudent to guarantee that a reduction of teaching load would automatically produce a great flowering of research. Yet this does not phrase the issue correctly. University policy should provide optimum conditions for research by those members of the faculty with the zeal and ability to engage in it. The quest for relief in teaching load should not be directed toward administrators only. Other colleges on this campus are governed by rules of their professional accrediting associations which set a ceiling on the number of teaching hours. Perhaps the Arts and Sciences should work toward a guild system.

Teaching and research conflict in yet another manner. Occasionally a faculty member secures a grant for research in Peru or Switzerland. When such grants are awarded to faculty members of the country's most prestigious institutions, his dean has no difficulty hiring a temporary replacement from a school lower on the academic totem pole. In most Deep South institutions the securing of a replacement is more difficult. This fact usually means that the courses handled by the wandering colleague will not be taught until his return. Possibly the university gains by this procedure, for the colleague returns better qualified in his field and with another publication to his credit. However, we should not deceive ourselves into thinking that the department's teaching program is not hurt while members of the staff are away. Or if an instructor secures a grant contingent on his being released half-time from teaching, the department's course offerings must be curtailed. Any administration that wishes its faculty to rise to the challenge of research should make clear that research has a high priority and that necessary sacrifices in other areas will be viewed with understanding.

If significant research is to be carried on in the Deep South, our universities must be able to recruit first-rate personnel to do this research. The prospects here are not encouraging. Low salary levels and the bad national image of Deep South states will not attract the ablest talent. Salaries of Deep South institutions are below the national average. One must have the greatest compassion for educational administrators who fight the good fight for increased funds.

They are like men on a treadmill. Since university salaries throughout the nation are rising, increased appropriations for our institutions leave them in about the same relative position.

Another aspect of the employment market is the increase in the number of universities that can offer salaries competitive with those of Deep South institutions. Occasionally, a colleague leaves the region for a better position at some institution you have never heard of. When you look up the school in an almanac, you find that until 1951 it was a teachers college or a municipal college or the agricultural college in a highly urban state. Now it is a full-fledged university with 9,000 students and an attractive salary scale.

Many Deep South institutions cannot begin to offer starting salaries that will attract people from the nation's top graduate schools. More and more, the region is going to be thrust on its own resources to hire talent. Here one must distinguish between the Deep South and the larger region that once constituted the Confederacy. Our best hope for recruiting able people is to get them from the best graduate schools in this region.

How did people communicate with each other before the expression "image" became so common? In any event, the Deep South has a bad public image. In the minds of many people it conjures up pictures of burning buses, snarling police dogs, and bombed churches. This image cannot be improved by arguing that a certain Ohio city has an even larger number of unsolved bombings than Birmingham. Nor will it help to argue that sin is not confined to the Deep South. So far as recruitment is concerned, this bad image stands in our doorway. Unhappily this is no morning-glory type of obstruction that wilts quickly in the afternoon sun, but a durable barrier that would turn away able people even if we had no salary problem.

Serious and ambitious research is financed with foundation money. A disturbing thought is that the region's bad image may influence those who control the purse strings of the great foundations. Here one casts discretion to the winds and operates on a purely speculative basis. Fifteen years ago the foundations regarded the South with compassion. We were underprivileged and virtuous. Where better could foundation money be spent than to uplift the virtuous poor? Today the white South represents sin. The reasoning goes something like this. Segregation is morally wrong; hence, those who live off segregationist taxpayers aid and encourage evil. No fine distinctions are drawn here. The same taxpayers feed southern social scientists and southern police dogs. Therefore, both groups must share the same attitudes. If either man or beast had an ounce of self-respect, he would leave the region and seek employment in a more moral environment. Or the dogs could retrain for seeing-eye responsibilities.

In the vocabulary of the psychiatrists a paranoiac is one who suffers from delusions of persecution. By imputing to a neutral or friendly environment all manner of non-existent hostility, he is enabled to avoid recognizing his own inadequacies. Possibly the speculation about foundation attitudes represents profound paranoia.

Our purpose is not to demonstrate that the obstacles confronting social science research in the Deep South are insurmountable. There is faith among many of us that first-class research and teaching in the social sciences can be done in the Deep South. Let us put an end to hand-wringing and consider our assets.

We have shattered a bottle of champagne on the one-and-one-quarter million dollar structure known as the Marten ten Hoor Hall. No one who has toured the building can hold that social scientists at the University of Alabama are ill-housed. The fact that the over-all length of the building exceeds that of a football field may offer proof to some that Alabama does not emphasize football above all else. Any visitor will be impressed with the private offices for all occupants and with the many special-purpose rooms, each tailored to the particular needs of the several departments. With respect to office equipment (computers, typewriters, dictating equipment, etc.) we are as well provided for as any institution in the entire South.

Another type of research asset is the University Research Committee. This committee has been in operation since 1943 and currently receives an annual allotment of $45,000 to be used for individual research grants to faculty members. Although grants are available to all departments on the campus, social scientists have always fared well at the hands of the committee.

Also aiding research is the University's Bureau of Public Administration. The Bureau's long record of research and publication includes some 60 studies published out of its own funds. In addition, there have been two dozen other studies where Bureau personnel did the research and funds for publication came wholly or in part from other sources. Akin to research were the answers to 1,365 requests for information from state and local officials received last year by the Bureau.

The presence of the Bureau is a research asset to the teaching staff of the Department of Political Science. Its publication program offers an outlet for studies produced by the department staff, and, to a limited degree, research can be encouraged by grants from the Bureau to Department members who are not otherwise employed in the summer. Moreover, the Bureau has administered research grants secured from other sources and has attracted certain grants because of its favorable national reputation. Finally, when the member of the teaching staff does any writing, the Bureau's secretarial staff is of great value.

The University's Office of Contract and Grant Development is another boon to research. If a faculty member can produce a well-thought-out research proposal, he can secure the services of the office in helping him to locate the foundation that would be most receptive to his proposal. In view of the astonishing number of foundations, some of them with specialized interests, the advice of a university officer knowledgeable of the world of foundations can be most advantageous.

The University has a serviceable library at present. Increased emphasis on research always makes exacting demands on libraries. Not only does it require complete collections of all manner of infrequently used materials but it calls for trained staff members who can locate technical material promptly.

Not all of our assets are tangible. An important asset has been a correct attitude on the part of the central administration toward research. The central administration does not require clearance of manuscripts, and no restraint is placed on the topics to be researched. This is significant since the publications of the Bureau of Public Administration, for instance, have not always avoided controversy. The two studies of apportionment of the Alabama legislature were not calculated to win praise from overrepresented sections of the state. The study *Government and Health* vexed the State Department of Health. *Registration of Voters in Alabama* noted that not all county boards of registrars rolled out the welcome mat for prospective Negro voters. *The Legislative Process in Alabama* was critical of the legislature, whence cometh our appropriations.

A final asset is the Deep South itself, which is a fascinating area for study by social scientists. While many southern social scientists will quite properly direct their attention to matters unrelated to the region, it is both an obligation and an opportunity for other social scientists to describe and interpret the process of the Deep South ceasing to be the Deep South. The region is struggling to enter the mainstream of American life but at a point pretty far upstream—approximately the Coolidge era. If this struggle accounts for so much that is tragic and frightening in southern life, let us recall that the greatest literature in political science has been written in times of turmoil.

Many aspects of southern life constitute research questions of considerable interest to social scientists. The contemporary South is the best area in the nation to study change in party allegiance. American states have changed party allegiance without many voters changing their minds. Michigan ceased to be solidly Republican in the early 1930's when a host of previously inarticulate non-voters were politically activated and entered the electorate as Democrats. Democrats are increasing in strength in traditionally Republican Maine and Vermont because of French-Canadian immigration. Only in the South do we find large numbers of long-time Democrats who are changing their party loyalty.

The South is a splendid laboratory for examining the role of violence in political power. This violence must not be confused with ordinary crime and homicide. In most democratic societies there is a constitutional consensus, that is, an agreement to disagree peaceably. Rarely does any minority group feel that its unique values have been so outraged that it resorts to violence or threats of violence to retain them. Only in the South in recent years has the value of law and order been considered debatable. The phrase "lie down and play dead" was a derisive expression for complying with federal court orders. Political scientists in the South can examine the conditions under which acts of political violence will or will not occur and the type of leadership that restrains them.

The South is the best place to study the behavior of judges under cross-pressures. Consider the situation of a United States District Court judge deciding a case involving school integration or Negro voting. His professional ties require him to follow the precedent of the higher courts. Yet if he does this, he may face anything from disapproval to social ostracism. His relatives back in Greenwood, Greenville, or Greensboro will not be able to understand what has come over him.

Or one might consider the decline of southern internationalism. The growth of local industry seems to have been associated with a declining enthusiasm for free trade. Religion and southern politics is an interesting area. Is the dogged faith in prohibition an unconscious mechanism by which we spare ourselves worry about weightier ethical matters? Or the southern preoccupation with states' rights could be used as a motivation to study federalism elsewhere in the world. Canada, Australia, Switzerland, and West Germany have federal type governments. Further study of their experience might offer new insights into our own.

Research on a large scale into the cause and meaning of the exciting events swirling around our doorstep is an expensive proposition that must be financed with grants from foundations. Most social science research grants of any size go to a small number of institutions at the top of the academic pyramid. Schools in the Deep South have no record for being the golden boys so far as receiving research money is concerned. Yet we can secure the needed funds only by assaulting the foundations more boldly. No one gets a foundation grant unless he applies for it. We have been less than zealous in the pursuit of locally available funds. Over the years there was no vigorous competition for University

Research Committee money until around 1958 when outside grants for the physical sciences became available contingent upon some local financial support. Nor have we been particularly aggressive in seeking outside aid. A correspondent in the Social Science Division of the National Science Foundation states: "In the past three fiscal years we have not received any [research] proposals from the state of Alabama." The writer goes on to suggest that my remarks "be directed toward encouraging your colleagues to consider formulating plans for the conduct of research." We need to submit more research proposals and have more rejected before we can feel underprivileged. In fact, it might be well to conclude these remarks by recalling the biblical parable of the unrighteous judge who finally granted the widow's request lest "she wear me out by her continual coming." The scriptural reference is included, not to question the righteousness of the foundations, but to exhort social scientists to imitate the secular shrewdness of the widow.

E. William Noland

Research Needs and Potentials

THE MAGIC WORD in social scientific research during the last fifteen years has been "interdisciplinary." The word means that often a social phenomenon is so multidimensional as to require the attention of representatives of not just one discipline, but of many. This makes sense. The failures we have suffered in this type of approach have not been due to error in this basic assumption concerning the need for such cross-fertilization and joint effort. Rather, most of the failure has been organizational, in communication breakdowns related to definition of terms, in lack of knowledge of the other person's discipline, and, in some instances, in sheer resistance to cooperation. Some pay only lip service to interdisciplinary research for they see in it a threat to the autonomy of their own discipline. Perhaps not until the need for substantial dovetailing of the social sciences is recognized, and accepted, will we have full-blown and productive interdisciplinary research. It is right here that the South provides us an image of opportunity.

Let us examine briefly the interdependence and complementarity of the social sciences by comparing the nature of my discipline, sociology, with that of others. Psychology is the study of processes going on within the organism—anxiety, emotion, reflexes, thinking. It involves the study of such phenomena as maturation, learning, motivation, perception. Sociology, where interaction is the key word, studies things going on between people—mutual impact, relations with one another. The two disciplines merge in social psychology, whose chief focus is the connection between interaction and internal individual processes.

Economics focuses on the results of human interaction on allocation of resources—land, labor, machinery, materials, money, other valued objects—and in their organization or efficient combinations. Sociology also is interested in the results of interaction. For instance, the effect of hostile communications on the cohesiveness or morale of a group illustrates the sociologist's interest in studying the impact of interaction on group characteristics. Also, a hypothesis claiming that pleasant and frequent contact with members of minority groups reduces the incidence of stereotypes and prejudice would reflect the sociologist's concern with the effect of interaction on values and beliefs.

The political scientist and sociologist also complement one another. Here the crucial concept of mutual interest is power. The political scientist studies the political institution per se; the sociologist examines the political institution as one of many. The focus of the political scientist is the state; of the sociologist, society. The political scientist is concerned principally with the positive and manifest functions of political institutions; the sociologist is more interested in social conflict and social change, in the informal and dysfunctional aspects of politics, and in latent institutional functions. But the common meeting ground for the two disciplines is clearly revealed when one examines some current problems in political sociology: voting behavior—does participation make for cleavage or consensus; politics of bureaucracy; internal government of voluntary organizations; and various concepts of power.

It seems fair to claim that the traditional historian studies particular events, while the theoretical historian compares events, indicates similarities and differences, and thus develops generalizations about processes. At this point, with the work of the theoretical historian, history and sociology converge. The sociologist is concerned with developing and confirming generalizations. For example, the traditional historian sees Eisenhower's election to the presidency as a unique event; the sociologist and the theoretical historian see Eisenhower's election to the presidency as a clue to hypothesize how voters make up their minds. The historian and the sociologist borrow from one another. The historian gets from the sociologist and other social scientists generalizations that help him in two ways: (1) these generalizations guide him in his selection of facts; and (2) they help explain the facts once selected. In the selection of pertinent facts, the historian needs a standard of relevance to ferret out proper items for attention. Such a standard of relevance may be a generalization from the social sciences. In explaining facts once selected, social science generalizations again come to the aid of the historian. For example, what modern economic theory has to tell us about the relation between the supply of precious metals and the price level enabled Keynes to attribute the rise of prices in Europe during the sixteenth and seventeenth centuries to the inflow of precious metals from America. Thus the laws of social science used to reconstruct the past are derived in the first place from studying contemporary social phenomena.

The dependence of the sociologist on the historian is equally dramatic; the former gets from the latter data for generalizations. The interdependence of the two is well illustrated in the work of Max Weber on the relationship between Protestantism and capitalism. As a historian, Weber studied the development of both phenomena in many countries; as a sociologist, he generalized to a relationship between the two in this fashion: Protestant beliefs and attitudes about hard work, thrift, and the importance of activities in the "here and now" led to the development of a new, capitalistic economic order.

In many respects sociology and social (or cultural) anthropology are growing into one discipline, with social interaction the central concept in such a dovetailing of foci. Anthropology is no longer considered to be the study of smaller, homogeneous, nonliterate societies. While Malinowski and Radcliffe-Brown saw in it the study of social interaction, other anthropologists, notably Americans, saw in their discipline the study of culture—behavior patterns, beliefs, artifacts, technology. Currently the interdependence of the two foci is becoming recognized.

Both the social sciences and the humanities study human social behavior. In fact, both often study rather specifically the same phenomena, but from different vantage points. Take, for example, the artist painting. To the teacher of painting, the most trenchant concerns are those of craftsmanship and aesthetics; the historian may be chiefly interested in changes in art form as reflectors of other types of change; the focus of the psychologist may be on the nature of creativity; the sociologist may look for the social role of the artist in a given society; and the economist may be reminded of the market for different kinds of artistic productions. Both history and literature reflect the past. Literature is often less rigorous and less factual than history, but it provides us one way of gaining insight into a society's culture at a given time.

The four-pronged work of the linguist illustrates significant meeting grounds for social science and the humanities. One aspect of linguistics is the study of language qua language.

Included here are descriptive, or structural, linguistics and comparative-historical linguistics. Here one gets involved in research that leads to propositions about languages, and about language as a distinctive category of behavior. Here the products are grammars, sound laws, theories of language, and the like. A second focus is the use of linguistic evidence in studies of culture history. Here linguistics provides additional data bearing on the history of a group or groups. Still another emphasis is the comparative study of language as a type of human behavior. This involves the comparison of linguistic systems qua systems to other systems, e.g., social structures, logical systems, and the like. The fourth linguistics prong consists of empirical studies of language use. This includes what is usually called psycholinguistics and socio- and anthropo-linguistics. This branch of linguistics studies such phenomena as the learnability and usability of this or that type of linguistic structure, where one encounters problems in communication, speech variation, language learning, and translation.

Social scientists use the specialized knowledge, insights and speculations provided by the humanists, but they strive to go beyond these to establish valid generalizations and theories which may lead to understanding and prediction. This last work, prediction, is the big differentiator. There is implied in the approach of the social scientist, using scientific methodology, an orientation predominantly to the future.

The natural sciences and the social sciences differ rather strikingly in ways besides the exactness with which they use the scientific method—or the ease with which the natural sciences raise money for research. Much natural scientific study focuses on things that are inanimate or non-human (e.g., in geology; animal husbandry). The work of the natural sciences on human beings (i.e., a part of zoology) focuses on the physiological aspects of man rather than the social (i.e., man in interaction with others). However, all people, including the most scientific of the scientists, work in a social context. Strictly speaking, man never works in isolation, and everyone's product is consumed by human beings, directly or indirectly. The interdependence of the social sciences and natural sciences is evident everywhere. In fact, perhaps nowhere are found better illustrations of the interdependence of all three—the social sciences, the humanities, and the natural sciences—than in the Aerospace Program.

Rocketry is the product of physics, chemistry, biology, engineering and physiological psychology. But the impact of the Aerospace Program is the concern of representatives of many other disciplines—all the social sciences, most of the other natural sciences, and even many of the humanities. In fact, almost any type of academic man should be able to find something of real interest in a careful examination of the social, economic, and political implications of the Aerospace Program. Let us try it now with only a cursory overview.

Already we have satellite-based communication systems for faster communication in diplomatic and international relations. Soon such systems will provide better control and management of far-flung business organizations, education of people in underdeveloped countries, and political manipulation to re-enforce relationships with friends and convert neutrals. When we get satellite-based weather prediction systems, there will follow attempts at weather control, better use of marginal food-raising areas, and the overcoming of tradition-bound methods of food raising.

From the Aerospace Program also will come many technological by-products. The practice of medicine is likely to be altered dramatically. New telemetering devices and complex data storage will provide us new ways of diagnosing disease. The doctor-patient-community-society relationship will be altered, perhaps especially medical economics. New fabricating materials—light, strong, non-corrosive, resistant to temperature extremes—are appearing, with community disruptions born of changes in labor skills, migration of people, and the displacement of old types of raw materials by new. Space research will modify the aircraft industry: there will be high speed shipment of freight as soon as we learn all we need to know about fitting commodities to space vehicles; aircraft lifting and braking rockets will permit airports to be smaller and remote areas to be served by jets.

The impact of the Aerospace Program on industry-government relations, a power struggle viewed by many as alarming, promises to be substantial. There are jurisdictional problems, such as the handling of patents, and the need to re-evaluate our present antitrust laws if a significant part of the financing is ever to fall into the private sector. Space industries proper, and even the supporting types, have difficulty by their very nature in financing themselves in the free private-enterprise sense. Dividends to stockholders are difficult to come by when the money is needed for research and development in such a rapidly changing technology. The product of our space industries is custom-made and limited in amount, the government is the chief consumer, there is no price mechanism, profits have to be negotiated, and a satisfactory scheme for computing performance efficiency is hard to find. Furthermore, the competition between government and private industry for scarce personnel, particularly high level scientists, is keen and, in the minds of some, controversial.

Many social scientists and humanists are raising questions these days concerning the possible impact of the Aerospace Program on the value system of our society. Some seem to be willing to argue that such values as personal achievement, individualism, freedom, and even efficiency have been reenforced, and that our seeming greater concern for reaching the moon than for feeding the poor has slowed the trend in the direction of our becoming an adjustment-oriented society, in favor of the old achievement-oriented one. And if we discover extraterrestrial life, is there not good reason to suspect that we shall modify substantially our conception of what man is capable of doing and our interpretation of certain biblical teachings?

Now let us turn to a basic question. Doubtless long before this, one has begun to wonder why I have devoted so much time to a discussion on the interrelatedness of the social sciences, the humanities, and the natural sciences. What has this to do with the central theme of the South as a laboratory for research? A great deal. Measured by teachers' salaries and expenditures per pupil, the South continues to suffer in the eyes of the nation. Despite the fact that changes in these two measures of attention to education reflect high relative improvement during the past decade and that many southern states spend a commendably high percentage of the tax dollar on education, the picture remains discouraging and in places even fuzzy. The situation with respect to emphasis on research is even worse. Coupled with a dearth of financial support for research has been the lack of conviction on the part of so many that it was essential. The natural sciences have fared the best in the South, but they have fared best everywhere. And the current situation is aggravated by the fact that foundations, for what they consider to be justifiable reasons, are not giving southern universities the attention they need. Consequently, the development of research in the South calls for a united front, hence my emphasis on the imperative that representatives of each discipline understand and be sympathetic toward the needs of others. Competition within a university for limited resources is good only to the point where it keeps each discipline aware of its needs; beyond this point, it can be devastating. Interdisciplinary research, in addition to its essentiality for handling properly certain types of propositions, can promote sympathetic understanding of one another's problems and optimum cooperation.

The battle between pure and applied research rages on. The purist looks down his large and sensitive nose at the unfortunate one who sells his soul on the throne of application. Almost in the same spirit as those who say, "He who cannot do, teaches," the pure researcher claims that "the inept theorizer and unsophisticated methodologist retires to the simple activity of counting noses without knowing why he is counting them, from which he counsels practitioners, often erroneously, on what to do." The purpose of research is to discover, to add knowledge, but it is not sinful per se to have that knowledge applied. Some educational institutions, especially the private ones, can afford current emphases on pure research. But the South must look substantially, if not chiefly, to its state-supported colleges and universities for its educational answers. Taxpayers (perhaps especially the less educated ones) like application—they want to know what education is good for; when you talk to them about research, they expect you to pinpoint the payoff. This is not to deprecate the work of private institutions which are not held as accountable, or that of institutions, most of which are outside the South, which can afford a full-blown pure research emphasis. In fact, they are to be emulated eventually. Most of the research we in America are sponsoring at the present time seems justified, and the South wants to carry its share of this load. However, if we are to arrive at that division of labor most conducive to educational progress in the South, we must face social, economic, and political facts realistically. In short, this is my belief: at the present stage of development of research in the South, many researchers cannot expect to find themselves for a while on the pure research pedestal; rather, they must be content to pass through an intermediate stage along the route, where the pure and the applied mingle freely and there is no quibbling about labels.

This intermediate stage needs further explanation. Perhaps, it would be easy for one to claim that I believe that no good pure research is being done in southern educational institutions. Nothing is further from the truth. Some research in the South compares very favorably with that being done elsewhere. But we need to talk in terms of averages. Facing squarely where we are now must not stay us from setting goals, from aspiring eventually to be numbered among the chosen. In fact, in this period of rapid change, it behooves us to regard self-evaluation, be it by a person, firm, region, or nation, as a continuous rather than as a periodic endeavor. There are many academic people in the South who are capable of doing outstanding research but have not had the chance to acquire the research habit, and a habit it is. These people can best get their feet wet with relatively simple beginnings. In this manner they can see their accomplishments, will not be discouraged, and will soon be willing and able to tackle that prestige-laden type of research called pure, with all its rights and privileges.

The big news these days is automation, or it should be. Someone has aptly called it the Second Industrial Revolution, for its impact is sure to be far-reaching and, if not handled properly, devastating. No region in our country can profit more from automation than the South, but no region is more vulnerable to its coming if the adoption is erratic. No phenomenon in our history cries louder for research attention. Most of what has been written about it to date is speculation.

As behavioral scientists, let us examine the human element

of this new technology. Will the job enlargement and job rotation automation is supposed to provide actually make jobs more challenging—or will the retraining demands be too burdensome and the higher intelligence levels which may often be required of workers too frustrating and tension-ridden? Will flatter organizations, providing fewer supervisory levels, a wider span of control, and theoretically better vertical communication because messages will not have as far to travel, prove to be more good than bad? Such organizational change is supposed to conduce to less close supervision, from which is to come morale- and character-building self-supervision by employees. How will the supervisor's job be altered in character: with automation permitting the writing of more and clearer standard operating procedures, will not the supervisor become more of an administrator? Will he become more a technical specialist and less a human relations expert, or vice versa? If the presence of fewer workers is to mean greater worker isolation at the work place, with what new challenge is the supervisor faced, what more can be learned about the relationship between a worker's background and what he expects of his job, and what may be the implications of such work space change for the labor union's function as a compensatory unifying and socializing force?

It seems reasonable that the trend toward the shorter work week will be speeded by automation. Is the argument that people of rural background—and the South has its share of these—are not as much concerned about the shorter work week as urbanites, a valid one? I doubt it. The country boy has had ample opportunity to learn city ways, and he has done it. Urban-rural differences in style of life have in large measure disappeared. All are equally interested in the leisure the shorter work week provides. But there may be significant differences in the way that leisure is spent. Communication technology makes city dwelling no longer a requirement for access to the cultural. In fact, there may be a significant negative correlation between degree of urbanism and opportunity for leisure to be spent purposively, in a way making for a greater capacity for work, achievement, and self-discipline. And always when one thinks in terms of one's spending his increased leisure in activities making for greater self-actualization, he encounters many questions begging for answers. For example, will the shorter work week, providing opportunity for the husband and father to be at home more, make for greater family stability? What will be the impact of such change on child-rearing patterns? Might there not emerge a substantially different basic family type?

Urban areas, particularly those outside the South, see in automation a boon to decentralization, especially in light of recent improvement in electric power transmission technology and the creation of light-weight fabricating materials. It appears that there likely will be less residential and business crowding, and the journey to work will take a shorter time and consequently be easier. Perhaps for the first time the choice between urban and suburban living will be a real one. But decentralization is not devoid of problems. Municipal governments will have new tax difficulties; renters of commercial properties in cities may be hit hard; spreading of population will create more work for the providers of goods and services. That the South will enjoy a distinct advantage over more highly urbanized regions in these respects appears to be a reasonable assumption, but it needs further examination. This is another trenchant research area.

Doubtless most people in the United States have been introduced to automation most dramatically by newspaper stories on its impact on employment. Some economists are able to present rather convincing evidence that as productivity increases unemployment diminishes, that technological change creates more jobs than it takes away, and that employment is negatively correlated with unit labor requirements. However, it would not be surprising if the attitude of the average American industrial worker toward automation runs something like this: "I am willing to believe that automation will cut direct labor costs, increase output, raise productivity, improve the quality of products, and create new types of industry—but what is it going to do to the job I have, and to that of my neighbor?" Probably most people can be divided roughly into two camps on the matter of the good and bad of automation relative to the over-all economy. It is not hard to find situations where the introduction of automated equipment has cost some workers their jobs, at least temporarily. This is predominantly true in the automobile, steel, communications, petroleum, electrical, banking, and insurance industries, where many or most of the operations are of the continuous flow type. But not all businesses will automate. Many do not lend themselves to it: some, such as mining and agriculture, can expect little more than a high level of mechanization, at least for a long time; some manufacture in lots of 25 or less; some have to redesign their products too frequently; and some will not be able to afford it.

High labor costs are one of the chief reasons for automating. I found during my recent year in Europe that one of the principal impediments to automation in many types of industries there was the remaining good supply of cheap labor, particularly that of Italians who were willing to migrate. By the same logic, other factors being equal, that region of this country with a significantly lower wage structure would automate least rapidly. But there is no such region; current interregional wage differentials are not sufficiently large to make a real difference in susceptibility to automation.

Perhaps automation's greatest disruption will be its effect on the wage structure of American business: companies which automate, despite the huge initial cost to which they will be subjected, will pay higher wages. Furthermore, it is claimed that automated industries will drain distressingly large amounts of capital from nonautomated ones, resulting in the layoff of workers and a decline in the capital labor ratio in the latter, with a concomitant decline in marginal productivity and wage rates. The negating argument here runs as follows: capital consuming automated firms will not absorb capital from other industries at a damaging rate or level; not all automated industries are capital consuming—some are capital saving; and the rate at which automation is likely to take place, largely because of its initial cost, will not be alarmingly fast.

I have just completed a study of fifteen factors which I have assumed to be associated with rate of growth of automation, in an effort to compare the six major regions into which this country is often divided on a type of adoption susceptibility scale. Ten of these factors were assumed to be positively associated with the growth of automation (e.g., per cent of work force which falls into the professional, technical, and kindred workers category; industrial diversification); the remaining five were adjudged to be impediments to its adoption (e.g., per cent of workers who are unskilled; per cent of total income coming from farms). Data for both 1950 and 1960 were used, to give a recent picture and a decade trend.

The results run as follows: To the extent that the 1960 values of these variables, taken together, are good predictors of the rate, by regions, at which automation will take place in our country, the South is in fifth place, being more advantageously situated than only one region, the Northwest. On the basis of this multi-factor measure, the Northeast will automate fastest, followed by the Midwest, the Far West, and the Southwest, in that order. However, when the 1950-60 trend is examined, the South moves into first place, with the Northwest, Southwest, Far West, the Northeast, and the Midwest following in that order. However, this finding should not create in southern proponents of automation great optimism, for the base from which improvement percentages are computed must be reckoned with. The South of 1950 had so far to go that its accomplishments during the 1950-60 decade, while substantial, must be viewed against the backdrop of what still remains to be done. When the two measures of automation susceptibility are combined, the South ties with the Midwest for fourth place, behind the Northeast, the Far West, and the Southwest, in that order. The Northwest was last, but the very nature of that region, unlike the South, is such as not to require an immediate serious look at automation.

So far, this discussion of the South as a research laboratory has described only some of those aspects of the new technology which have most direct relevance to this region and its appropriate focus on research—modification of job types at all organizational levels and, consequently, worker qualifications; the shorter work week, with its implications for leisure spending; the good and bad of decentralization, with degree of urbanization an important variable; and the impact of automation on employment, the wage structure, and the total economy. I have deliberately postponed until now what is possibly the most important single consideration of all: the training and retraining of workers, calling for a dramatic redesigning of our educational system.

Now I submit a proposition which may represent a striking departure from the usual thinking about automation and the type of educational training it requires. I predict that in many underdeveloped countries about to industrialize, a degree of automation will be reached that will compare favorably with ours but in much less time. Many of the steps through which we have passed in arriving at our present state of technology will be by-passed. The education of the work force in such countries at a given point in time can be patterned to the technology extant. If this is true, may we not claim the same process occurring in the less industrialized segments of this country, in which parts of the South figure rather dramatically? If this is true, the South, or important parts of it, can engage in a considerable amount of educating directly for the automated age. There will be less unlearning of old work habits than will be found in the more highly industrialized regions. The farm boy will not have to learn mechanized and semi-automated jobs if highly automated ones are present begging for his services. All this opens up a whole new area for educational and sociological research—what new things need to be taught, and what can be omitted. Let us briefly consider a few researchable educational problems of special relevance to the South at the present time.

In many respects it appears that the southern family has played a more important role in the socialization of the child than the nonsouthern family. Perhaps, then, the southern school has played a less important socialization role than have schools elsewhere. This may point up an urgent need for education to assume a more prestigeful place in the thinking of southern youngsters and their parents, if the new technology is to be learned expeditiously. Book learning will have to be emphasized more. Optimum balance between family socialization and school socialization is an important question for the South. Research must come up with the answer.

A pattern of distribution of teachers by sex has developed in American education. Women teachers predominate and, in fact, are found almost exclusively in certain types of teaching. Apparently men are considered better for other types. But is there a meaningful rationale for all this, or is it simply the result of chance, whim, and strange stereotyping? The new education calls for an examination of this sex preference question. It is a researchable phenomenon the South can well afford to tackle.

When one examines the purposes of education, he often arrives at three: the inculcation of moral values; the emotional, social, and intellectual development of the child, often with no clearcut notion of the division of labor among the three; and indoctrination in the acceptance of the status quo. With respect to educating for new types of jobs, the time has arrived to challenge the status quo everywhere. The school system in the South is among the most vulnerable in this educational focus; it must quickly discover what changes should be made and how to bring them about.

There are such substantial differences between elementary and secondary schools in organization and structure that one often wonders about the impact on the child of transition from one to the other and, if serious, just what can be done about it. Also, in much the same fashion, one wonders about the good and bad of school centralization. Research on optimum size and complexity of school unit is a type in which the South can profitably engage, for it is currently in the position of having to build many new schools if it is to keep educational pace with the remainder of the nation.

Another area of real concern as a region faces major redesigning of its educational sytem is the seeming lack of congruency between the students' definition of the teacher's role and the teacher's definition of his own role. Add to this confusion the distinct possibility that parents and the community at large have additional definitions of the teacher's role which are not consistent with one another or with that of teacher or pupil, and there results a dilemma probably related to such current educational impediments as student dropouts, parental indifference, hesitancy on the part of many potentially fine teachers to enter that profession, and community nonsupport of education.

Support of education by a community inevitably is tied in with the economic, educational, and religious composition of that community and its power structures. Some will argue that a community of like people will cooperate well, while others insist that heterogeneity of population is functional in that the competition that resides in such heterogeneity is needed to get important things done. The South, currently far less homogeneous than just a few decades ago, needs to learn how it can best handle this greater population diversification in building its educational program.

In the life of the school teacher in America, rewards, requirements, and expectations have long been out of kilter. Many high school principals are lucky if they receive as much salary as the industrial shop foreman, but think of the difference between them relative to what that salary must pay for. How to enhance the prestige of teaching, how to make it a sought-after profession, is a problem begging for meaningful research. Actually we know little of the dynamics of membership in the teaching profession: who enters it, and who remains in it. A very large percentage of our teachers are of middle class origin, a fact which may make it difficult for them to understand and establish rapport with the students of lower class origin, who often constitute a substantial segment of their classes. What constitutes promotion? Is it not too often true that the only visible accouterment of recognition for a teacher is his becoming an administrator? The whole problem of how the teaching profession can become more nearly a true profession is crucial but researchable. And nowhere is there a greater need to study this problem, or more opportunity to do so, than in the South.

In this picture of the South relative to its research needs and potentials four major points have appeared: (1) representatives of all academic disciplines should forget their differences, recognize their interdependence, help one another raise money, and join hands in actually doing interdisciplinary research when such a type is most feasible; (2) these same representatives of all disciplines should acquire a stronger belief in the merits of research than they have now, see it as an important if not essential adjunct of good teaching, but not quibble, at least for the present, over whether it is pure or applied; (3) the South should recognize that it is at that stage industrially where anything less than the proper facing up to automation, through a strong research and development effort, can be disastrous, but where the right kind of attention can work wonders; and (4) a dramatic reworking of the educational system is necessary, with guidelines to be provided, again, by serious and imaginative research.

Please note the solid thread of optimism throughout my remarks. Perhaps one such as I, who was so long identified with the South, could not have done otherwise. But this is not sheer sentimentality. I am convinced that the New South, which to some has not yet come and to others has been too long in arriving, is emerging. With diligence here and a timely concession there, the South can soon arrive at that stage Dr. Edwin Anderson Alderman, President of the University of Virginia the early part of this century, doubtless had in mind when he predicted a crop of southerners "trained to observe closely, to imagine vividly, to reason accurately, and to have about them some humility and some toleration."

At another point in Dr. Alderman's address, "The South's

Real Problem," he writes: "Twenty years from now [it was then 1906] the old patriarchal South will be a fierce industrial region. By industrialism I do not mean commercialism. Commercialism is a mere sordid theory of life. Industrialism is the scientific mastery of the raw material and its wise distribution according to the laws of trade. Thus considered, industrialism is a mighty and moral part of the movement of society. When the practice of industrialism catches up with the spirit, politics will be nationalized and thought liberalized in the South, for the economic structure of society is largely responsible for its ideals. Our real problem, therefore, is to try to industrialize our society, without commercializing its soul. I wonder if the thing is possible?" The thing is possible, Dr. Alderman.

THE DEEP SOUTH IN TRANSFORMATION

Its Development,
Past and Present

Rembert W. Patrick

The Deep South, Past and Present

EVERY SURVEY of the South begins with a question. Answering that question—what is the South?—is the imperative task of the historian or the scholar in any other discipline. Those who attempt to account for the distinctiveness of the South seek answers in causation which range from definable climate to indefinable mystique. Inevitably these investigators reach common conclusions, namely, that a unified, monolithic South is a myth and that there are many "Souths" instead of just one South.

Even more difficult than delineating the Old South is defining the modern South. Today, the contrasts between Miami and Bonifay, Florida, are as marked as the differences between New York City and Centreville, Alabama. Whatever the historical period considered, "South" is more realistic than South. In speech and writing, however, there is a region of the United States known as the South.

Although describing a part of this mythical South is less difficult than identifying the whole, there is no satisfactory answer to the question: "What is the Deep South?" Physical similarity offers one explanation of the Deep South. Most of its land is low and flat, watered by abundant rainfall, and drained by a network of rivers which flow into the Atlantic or the Gulf of Mexico. Each of its six states* borders on the sea, four of them on the Gulf, and a fifth, Georgia, has an outlet to

* Alabama, Florida, Georgia, Louisiana, Mississippi, and South Carolina.

the Gulf by the Chattahoochee-Flint-Apalachicola waterway; three of the states have long coastlines on the Atlantic Ocean. The summers often seem interminable, the heat unendurable. The winters are mild; the humidity is high but the days of sunshine are numerous. On the average the growing season for crops lasts for nine months. On the other hand, there are notable variations in physical characteristics. The Appalachian highlands of the northern area have a maximum altitude of 3,500 feet in South Carolina, rise to 4,784 in Georgia, and descend gradually until they disappear in Mississippi. The rolling hills of the Piedmont extend south to the 325 foot high Iron Mountain of peninsular Florida. There are waterpower sites in some areas, minerals in others, and oil deposits in still others. Natural lakes, swamps, and bayous dot the landscape. Winter temperatures range from subzero to forty degrees above zero.

Physically the region is one of similarities and contrasts, but geography has not determined the civilization of the Deep South. According to Rupert B. Vance, history has given the South its distinctive characteristics, and his statement is more applicable to the Deep South than to the entire region. Notwithstanding a dedication to the status quo in many aspects of their culture, white and colored southerners have lived and are living in a changing South. Variation in the use of natural resources, technological development in agriculture and industry, and alteration in philosophy have repeatedly modified the culture of a people.

The Deep South has unique historical features. The flags of five governments have flown over the region—Spain, France, England, the United States, and the unrecognized Confederate States of America. Prior to the Civil War the six states of the Deep South concentrated on the production of staple money crops—cotton, sugar cane, and rice. These states were the most rural of all the so-called sovereign states of the Union. In 1860 Louisiana's 26 per cent urban population was percentage-wise ten times larger than Mississippi's 2.6 per cent. In whole numbers the rural population of the other four states was: Alabama, 95; Florida, 95; Georgia, 93; and South Carolina, 93. In racial composition these states ranged from 60 per cent Negro in South Carolina to 44 per cent in Georgia, and the total population of the six states was 50.4 per cent white and 49.6 per cent Negro.

These Deep South states were the first ones to withdraw from the Union. Before the arrival of Texans at Montgomery, delegates of these revolutionary states had established a provisional southern government and selected a president and a vice president. Throughout the Confederacy, sons of the Deep South occupied most of the executive offices of the rebel government. The presidency, vice presidency, and half of the cabinet positions were monopolized by sons of the Deep South. In addition cabinet members Robert Toombs, Leroy Pope Walker, and Thomas Hill Watts came from the region.

After the Civil War white citizens of these states were less willing than other southerners to accept the cultural implications of military defeat. The "Black Codes" of Mississippi, South Carolina, Louisiana, and Florida rigorously and unreasonably proscribed the freedmen to a second class citizenship. When checked by a legal government, supported by a majority of the voters, the white minority used lawlessness and economic intimidation to defeat democratic processes. Flagrant illegalities forced federal action and extended Congressional Reconstruction in Florida, Louisiana, and South Carolina to 1877.

Once in control of their state governments, white conservatives relied on fraud to negate the vote of the Negro and white opposition. With the passage of time, the nation abandoned the Negro, leaving him to the care of his former master who established a caste system and devised constitutional provisions and state laws acceptable to a United States Supreme Court whose justices were more interested in upholding property rights than in protecting human rights. The Deep South not only led its region in the passage of Jim Crow legislation but also in mob action to insure white supremacy. Perhaps because they doubted the efficacy of laws and courts to sublimate the Negro, these southerners blackened their region's reputation with lynchings and other extra-legal actions. Furthermore, most Americans associated the Deep South with peonage and the chain gang as well as poverty, disease, and ignorance. Politicians Theodore Bilbo, Cole L. Blease, Tom Heflin, and "Cotton Ed" Smith became symbols of the bigotry and racism of southerners. Although the Ku Klux Klan was a national disgrace, the stronghold of this organization was the Deep South. In the twentieth century, whenever possible white southerners gave no more than surface compliance to Supreme Court decrees relating to racial matters.

Maintaining white supremacy either by slavery or the caste system has been a consistent policy, but in other respects the Deep South has experienced revolutions. Tractors have replaced mules, cultivators have conquered hoes, and diversified agriculture has won over the single crop economy. Industry and services have relegated agriculture to a secondary status. Hookworm, malaria, and other debilitating diseases have been almost eradicated. Increased productivity has brought balanced diets, comfortable houses, and good clothing for most of the people. Such heavy blows have been dealt illiteracy that this critical problem of yesteryear requires less attention today than do adequate facilities for high school and college students.

In 1960 the city instead of the farm was characteristic of the Deep South. Only Mississippi with 63 per cent and South

Carolina with 59 per cent rural inhabitants were agrarian. Seventy-three per cent of Floridians, 63 per cent of Louisianans, 54 per cent of Alabamians, and 55 per cent Georgians resided in cities. Florida's urban population was 5 per cent higher than the national average. Between 1950 and 1960 Mississippi lost 214,000 rural residents while gaining 213,000 urban ones. Urban communities in South Carolina attracted 203,000 people compared with 62,000 for rural places. Within a century the population of the Deep South shifted from 90 per cent rural to more than 50 per cent urban.

The recency of this change has political significance. Florida became urban in the 1930's, Louisiana in the 1940's, and Alabama and Georgia in the 1950's. The majority of southern urbanites are less than a generation removed from a farm environment. Although living in cities, these people retain rural attitudes; a mere scratch will disclose the farm base under their city veneer. As yet they do not realize that their interests and needs differ from those of their rural cousins. Compared to the financial status of their progenitors, southern urbanites enjoy affluence. As a result of this sudden increase in their standard of living, and of the quickness of the population shift from country to city, these people support conservative politicians who give lip service to laissez-faire economic principles while pushing government aid to business and placing the burden of taxation on the common man. City people have not attained sufficient unity to force their legislators to give them equitable representation in state assemblies or in the United States House of Representatives.

In racial composition the Deep South has also experienced revolutionary change. The nearly 50 per cent Negro population of 1860 was reduced to 29 per cent a century later, when in density the Negro population ranged from 42 per cent in

Mississippi to 18 per cent in Florida. Although the Negroes were not the majority in any Deep South state, their numbers were unevenly distributed within every state. Hence, they constituted a majority in some counties. In 1960, 32 per cent of the almost 19,000,000 Negro citizens of the nation resided in the Deep South. The number of Negroes in the region and the determination of white southerners to dominate them has always been the most potent factor in making the Deep South a unique region.

Among modern romanticists are many rabid segregationists who, judged by their speeches and writings, believe American civilization attained its apex before the Civil War. Their conception of the Old South is a blending of myth, romance, and fact. History forces them to admit that only two states of the Deep South belonged to that select circle of states which united to establish the United States of America, but in their opinion later political units created by the federal government attained sovereignty upon admission into the Union. According to these romanticists the southland was peopled by cavaliers of England whose descendants dotted the Deep South with white-columned mansions. Living in these were a cultured, hospitable people, burdened only with the care of childlike, contented slaves. The racially superior white man uplifted the inferior Negro, who worked under a benign master and enjoyed the most comprehensive social security system ever devised by man. From the joint production of happy slaves and responsible managers, the master class gave the laborer the necessities of life and used the remainder in a gracious living, known as the "southern way of life." Instead of racial conflict there was harmony and mutual respect, with every person knowing and keeping his ordained place in society. If the white man contributed little to the creative arts, he enjoyed the best in literature and excelled in the forensic and political arts.

What are the facts? There were at least five social classes in the Deep South: the free Negro, the slave, the poor white trash, the yeoman, and the planter-aristocrat. In origin most of the white people were the descendants of poor European immigrants. The ancestors of the Deep South southerners were so poor that they could not pay their passage to America. Like the first Negro immigrants they were indentured servants who agreed to serve a predetermined number of years in return for transportation across the Atlantic. Freedom and opportunity were the inducements given to white and Negro alike, but these rewards for faithful service soon became the exclusive right of white people. Because of the color of his skin the Negro's term of service was lengthened to life and his child's inheritance was slavery. There was no disgrace in being the sons of white indentured servants; on the contrary, the advancement of these people testified to their ambition and industry, and to the opportunities in America. Whatever the desire for freedom, whatever the ability and industry possessed by the Negro, these were suppressed by the laws of the white majority. Consequently, the two largest social classes that settled and developed the Deep South were the Negro slave and the yeoman white, the latter having opportunity and the former being denied it by law.

The economic and social order of the Deep South was complex for a primarily agrarian society. Most numerous were the slaves while the free Negroes composed the smallest class. There were many gradations in occupation and social position within these classes. Among the slaves were domestic servants and skilled artisans, foremen and field-hands; the free Negroes ranged from wealthy, slaveowning planters to poverty-stricken, unskilled laborers. In 1860 more than 250,000 "free persons of color" resided in the entire South; but less than 37,000 of these lived in the Deep South, almost 30,000 of whom were in Louisiana and South Carolina. Only 932 Negroes in Florida and 773 in Mississippi were allowed a second class citizenship, the lot of all free Negroes in the United States.

Numbers can only be estimated for the white classes of the Deep South. The demarcation line between the poor whites and the yeoman and the yeoman and the planter-aristocrat cannot be determined. Although the farmer and the planter loomed largest in the yeoman and planter-aristocrat classes, the designations are semantical nomenclature. According to the 1860 census, the planters of Louisiana outnumbered those of any other Deep South state, but there were more clerks than planters in the pelican state. The 907 barkeepers of Louisiana and the 201 of Alabama are indicative of the hundreds of non-farmers included in the yeoman class. Doctors, lawyers, professors, hotel keepers, merchants, and bankers as well as large land and slaveowners belonged to the planter-aristocracy. Certainly the non-slaveowning yeomen were numerically the largest white class in the Deep South and the poor whites the smallest.

The ownership of slaves and acres, however, was the goal of ambitious men. In popular opinion these evidences of wealth somehow endowed their possessors with an aura of culture and political acumen. Did they? There were educated aristocrats in the Deep South and wealthy illiterates; there was a gracious society and a crude society, depending upon the individuals involved. There were benign masters and cruel ones; there were strong bonds of affection between slaves and masters as well as deep-rooted hatreds. Always the white people had a gnawing fear that the slave would rebel against his legally enforced status. This fear expressed itself in many ways: by the deletion in newspapers of every reference to the fighting ability of Negroes, by the repressive laws passed after slave uprisings, by the use of religion both to frighten the Negro and offer him eternal rewards, and by the patrol system to keep the slaves under control. While astute owners appealed to the loyalty and pride of their slaves, or gave their laborers gifts and leisure to stimulate effort, the institution of slavery was perpetuated by law and lash. It stripped human dignity from almost half of the people and debased many of the others.

If the peculiar social and economic systems of the Deep South had produced a golden age of literature and fine arts, modern man would have some reason to justify their existence. But the best tribute to the enlightened southerners is to say that they were the consumers instead of creators of the arts. The residents of two states participated in and contributed to the revolutionary and early national periods of the United States, the golden ages of the South. Despite the novels of William Gilmore Simms and the poems of Paul Hamilton Hayne, the literary production of Deep South southerners can be dismissed except for the earthy humor of Augustus B. Longstreet and Joseph G. Baldwin. Unfortunately many modern Negroes reject the outstanding achievement of that age: the pleadings in spirituals and folksongs of a people yearning for freedom.

Knowledgeable apologists for the cultural desert which was the Deep South emphasize the region's short life span. They make a point that is frequently overlooked. "Old South" often implies a long existence, but in reality the antebellum Deep South endured for only one generation. In the eighteenth century fortunes were made in rice and indigo on the coastal lands of South Carolina and Georgia, but the cotton and sugar kingdoms of the Deep South belonged to the third through the sixth decade of the nineteenth century. Louisiana had been a state forty-nine years before it seceded and Florida was in the Union for less than sixteen years. The span of time requisite for creativeness in the arts was, therefore, largely the figment of imagination. In the fluid society of the Deep South, human energy was mainly utilized in acquiring property and the social status associated with wealth.

The economic backgrounds of prominent southerners support this contention. Jefferson Davis came from yeoman stock. Vice president of the Confederacy, Alexander H. Stephens, and three cabinet members, Judah P. Benjamin, Christopher G. Memminger, and Stephen R. Mallory, rose from poverty or orphanhood to economic affluence. William Gilmore Simms was poor until his second wife's father provided him security, and John C. Calhoun was aided by perceptive South Carolinians. If the skin of the ambitious man were white and if he had ability, the doors of Deep South mansions were open to him.

To retain his status he had to conform to the ideological tenets of the master class. Southern womanhood had to be praised, and, if necessary, defended. Following the preaching of orthodox ministers was essential. To question the literal interpretation of the Bible, or to doubt God's endorsement of slavery, endangered one's earthly and celestial home. Above all a responsible member of society was obligated not only to uphold the institution of slavery but also to detail its virtues.

Deep South southerners possessed admirable characteristics but their prowess as public speakers and statesmen is a myth. Years before secession, orators had run out of ideas. Their voices were good, their gestures were pleasing, and their speeches were embellished with quotations from classical literature, but in content reason yielded to emotion and invective. By their own words southerners admitted their political ineffectiveness. In a single paragraph they lauded themselves or their ancestors for political leadership and condemned a federal government which favored the North and discriminated against the South. John C. Calhoun had a rare ability to describe and analyze a problem, but little talent for solving it. When his theory of nullification proved unacceptable, the Deep South turned to state sovereignty and secession. Extraneous argument and meaningless theories glossed the essential reason for disunion, the defense of an antiquated way of life based on slavery. In an age of nationalism and freedom, southern politicians demonstrated their lack of prescience by adhering to provincialism and defending human bondage.

Secession was the most costly political blunder in American history. It brought on a war which cost the lives of 600,000 men and left other thousands wounded in body and mind. Billions of dollars worth of property was destroyed. The advocates of state sovereignty endured more centralization under their own Confederate government than they had dreamed possible under federal rule. However beneficial nationally, emancipation confiscated most of the accumulated capital of southerners. Failure in battle broke the spirit and wrecked the economy of the Deep South.

The unexpected leniency of the victor quickly revived southerners and gave them hope of winning the peace. They accepted reunion, the original northern purpose of the war, in good faith, but neither admitted war guilt nor completely repudiated the idea of state sovereignty. Although some legislators held that the Thirteenth Amendment made redundant the outlawing of slavery in state constitutions, southerners recognized that slavery belonged to history. They were unwilling, however, to give freedmen equality under law. Sometimes referred to as the third objective of the Civil War, equality was more the product of peace than of the battlefield. The legislators of Mississippi and South Carolina, therefore, were amazed by northern reaction to their "Black Codes."

In a rare demonstration of political awareness, Mississippians repealed the more obnoxious provisions of their code, but Floridians reflected the real southern sentiment by defying northern opinion. Before the Florida legislators began consideration of a black code, they were fully cognizant of the northern attitude. Despite this fact, the legislature accepted a report which praised slavery as the best economic institution devised by man, criticized the institution only for its failure to regulate properly the sex activities of Negroes, and proceeded to enact a series of discriminatory laws. Florida's action was indicative of southern resurgence and a determination both to resist the demands of "do-gooders" and to give the freedmen no more than a second class citizenship.

Probing the reasons for the fiasco which was Reconstruction has been an interesting pastime. Perhaps the emotionalism of the postwar era prevented a reasoned approach to difficult problems. Even without the conquered's defiance of the conqueror, or without an uncompromising, politically inept man in the White House, Congress may have repudiated presidential reconstruction and assumed control. The historian, however, is confronted with the facts of presidential reconstruction, congressional reconstruction, and the southern determination to maintain white supremacy.

Certainly the reconstruction era cries for more study. The myths surrounding it, especially those associated with the Deep South, should be separated from actuality. Southerners have legitimate reason for condemning a political indecision which gave them hope for reprieve in presidential reconstruction and then attempted to enforce the principle of first class citizenship regardless of race under congressional reconstruction. Undoubtedly, the southern Republican governments were corrupt. The desire of Deep South southerners to establish and maintain white supremacy cannot be denied. The political base of Deep South Republican governments was the Negro voter.

After recognizing these facts, without passing judgment on them, the investigator runs into myths. The first of these is the reputed harshness of congressional reconstruction. The fact is that never in history have the defeated in a civil war received so light a sentence as did southerners in 1867. Under congressional reconstruction not a single man was executed or imprisoned for rebellion, and not an acre of land or a penny's worth of other property belonging to the vanquished was confiscated. The second myth claims that thirty or more per cent of southerners were disenfranchised. In fact only those who could not take the iron-clad oath were denied the franchise in selecting delegates to constitutional conventions and in recording their acceptance or rejection of the proposed constitutions. Either Negro constitution-makers or Negro voters refused to deny the franchise to their white brothers. The Fourteenth Amendment prevented many former confederates from holding state and federal office, but did not interfere with the voting privilege of these people. A third myth describes a southern society as inverted with the bottom rail placed on top. In no Deep South state, even South Carolina with its Negro majority in the legislature, did the freedmen control the government. Politically, economically, and socially the white people retained primacy over the Negroes. A fourth myth indicts the freedmen for their lawlessness, but in reality conservative white men resorted to nihilism to subjugate the freedmen.

Southerners who condemn the post World War I Ku Klux Klan and praise the klan and other terrorist organizations of the post Civil War period handle truth lightly. Except for a few years of juvenile antics, the klan was a vicious organization. Even the pro-southern historian E. Merton Coulter has declared that the klan "left a heritage which was to bedevil and disgrace the South thereafter, as mobs took the law into their own hands and engaged in barbarous lynchings—unjustified under any code of civilized rule." Furthermore, the claim that terrorism speeded the restoration of white political supremacy in the Deep South is questionable. Lawlessness necessitated federal action to protect citizens from assault. In my opinion, the illegal activities of klan members and like-minded terrorists extended the life of Republican governments in the Deep South.

These illustrations point out some of the mythology surrounding the southern phase of Reconstruction without detailing other realities. The post Civil War period was an age of national as well as local corruption. No Deep South government swindled its taxpayers of as much money as the Tweed Ring grabbed from residents of New York City. In the South the Negro's ill-gotten gain was miniscule in comparison with that of the white carpetbagger, white scalawag, or white conservative. Historians should give more attention than they have to ideological changes which multiplied the services of state and local governments and consequently required the collection of more taxes and the expenditure of larger sums of money. And the achievements of Deep South Republican regimes should not be overlooked: the excellence of state constitutions, the widening of political democracy, economic and social reforms, and educational progress. Instead of being the terminal date of Reconstruction, 1877 more accurately marks the beginning of the southern-dominated phase of that misunderstood era.

During the fifteen years following the Civil War the Deep South gained political power in the United States House of Representatives. In 1860 the region's six states sent twenty-eight men to the House or 11.5 per cent of its total. Despite enlargement of the Union by the admission of five states and the phenomenal increase of population in frontier areas, in

1880 the Deep South had forty men or over 12 per cent of the members of the House. A literal application of Section 2 of the Fourteenth Amendment would have reduced representation from the Deep South, but by 1880 southerners were winning a part of the peace.

A combination of factors gave the South partial victory. The northern people tired of the seemingly eternal Negro question. Accepting social Darwinism, they judged and condemned the former slave who had not utilized freedom to prove himself a superman. Needing southern votes in the Congress, northern industrialists and politicians sacrificed Negro rights for material wealth. Newspaper and magazine editors welcomed the articles of writers who sympathized with the misjudged and downtrodden South. A mythical Old South floated cloud-like from the past to cover the ills of the New South. Public opinion supported white southerners, not the colored ones; and swayed by that opinion, the Supreme Court rendered decisions which made possible legal discrimination.

At the same time a resurgent imperialism turned nations toward the undeveloped regions of the world. Industrialist and intellectual, politician and patriot accepted the white southerner's contention that there were inferior and superior races. Exporting his superior civilization to the racially inferior peoples of Africa and Asia became the white man's burden. In the twentieth century senators and representatives who voted millions of dollars to kill islanders in the Philippines could only shed crocodile tears for Deep South Negroes. The caste system was condoned in the South and imitated in the North. In racial affairs southerners enjoyed the pleasant midstream waters of American history.

In domestic and foreign affairs, many twentieth century southerners were stalwart advocates of progressive measures. During the New Freedom of President Wilson and the

New Deal of President Roosevelt, Deep South congressmen gave essential votes for legislation to better or to bolster the capitalistic system of the United States. The Federal Reserve System, credit for farmers, federal aid to education, relief measures, the Tennessee Valley Authority, social security, wage and hour laws are some of the domestic acts, now proven worth-while by experience, which southerners supported. In foreign affairs, they foresaw that Imperial and Hitler's Germany threatened the world balance of power. Southerners voted for reciprocal trade agreements and aided in changing the Monroe Doctrine from a unilateral policy of the United States to a multilateral policy of the American republics. They welcomed a plan for the peaceable solution of international problems through the United Nations and supported every move to assail or contain communism. Before the court of public opinion a strong case can be made for the progressivism of the Deep South.

Within their territorial boundaries, these states attacked critical problems with statesmanship. The needs of citizens living in an increasingly complex society were recognized by giving local and state governments regulatory and service powers. Even a listing of reforms, an enumeration of material and ideological advances, would tax the patience of listener and reader. These innovations limited capricious and predatory individualism, but, in result, they helped to give Deep South residents a higher standard of living and more opportunity than they or their ancestors had ever enjoyed.

In human relations some southerners worked to ease the burden placed upon Negroes. Hands were shaken; last names were used and Miss, Mr., or Mrs. placed before them; efforts were made to pronounce Negro correctly; and the first letter of that word was capitalized. These were not unimportant concessions by white southerners with deep-rooted prejudices. Various forms of discourtesy were and still are the psychological weapons of racial discrimination. Like Thomas Jefferson did in the wisdom of age, liberal southerners realized that environment, not heredity, was the principal reason for the lowly station of the Negro. Still they shuddered at "Uncle Tomism" without acknowledging their part in forcing the Negro into a degrading obeisance. They took care of "their Negroes," excused their faults and protected them from their would-be tormentors, but seldom treated them with the dignity desired by human beings. Southerners eased throbbing consciences by imitating the Christ-approved act of the Good Samaritan, never admitting that the teachings of Jesus encompassed both relieving the sufferer and attacking the cause of his distress.

As the twentieth century advanced, the opportunities and rights of Deep South Negroes increased. Though remaining relatively inferior, Negro schools gave educational advantages to youths and teaching positions to adults. By serving their own people, many Negroes achieved financial success in business and the professions. During the New Deal and subsequent years the Negro shared in the national economic betterment. His buying power forced sales-conscious white merchants to treat him with some respect.

Deep South southerners and outsiders were responsible for elevating the Negro. While many southerners protested against outside criticism of or interference with their local institutions, the Supreme Court rendered decisions because southern officials refused to give equal protection under the law to a minority under their jurisdiction. Local and state governments of the Deep South responded in different ways to court orders: some complied, but others used subterfuge to delay enforcement or contravene the intent of court decrees. In some places Negroes served on juries, rode on integrated interstate carriers, registered and voted; in other localities hastily enacted laws, variation in interpretation of laws, police power, and prejudiced courts were relied on to maintain the caste system.

Following the *Brown* v. *Board of Education* decision in 1954, white southern opposition against outside interference erupted. The do-nothingism of the national administration, as well as the failure of middle-class southerners to support law and order, allowed the lawless and the legal "befuddler" to control the Deep South. Unfortunately the national spotlight focused on the wielders of bats and clubs, who attempted to maintain segregation by force, and on the dramatic acts of governors, who were no more successful in preventing token integration in educational institutions than a ruler of ancient times was in commanding tidal waters to be still.

As degrading as were these demonstrations, the most serious indictment of Deep South leaders was their intellectual paucity. In defense of caste they resorted to Old South reasonings for the continuation of slavery. Southern politicians resurrected nullification, the most colossal political failure of the Old South's most famous political scientist. No southern state other than his own supported John C. Calhoun's idea; even in South Carolina opponents of the "nullies" raised American flags and armed themselves to resist the nullifiers. Yet twentieth century southerners relied on this discredited idea to maintain racial discrimination. After failing, they returned to the successful methods employed by their post Reconstruction ancestors: interpreting laws in one way for white people and in another for Negroes, using the police power of the majority to cow the minority, and depending on juries to give more consideration to the color of skin than to evidence.

It would be foolhardy to predict the Deep South's future on the basis of its past. History belongs more to the humanities than to the exact sciences. Historians cannot be truly objective for their sphere is humanity—men and women with fears, prejudices, superstitions, and expectations. The interpretations of historians are conditioned by environment, and truth, however sought after, is illusive. The conscientious historian can do no more than detail and interpret ancestral successes and failures and apply intelligence in suggesting future actions.

On these bases one foresees tremendous possibilities for the Deep South. The region is endowed with a pleasant climate, bountiful resources, and a favorable location. It has the human resources requisite to remarkable achievement. The economic achievements of one generation have demonstrated the region's potential. But with regard to freedom, the Deep South remains the nation's number one problem. If it can shed narrow provincialism, liberate itself from retarding prejudices and superstitions, create a society in which the exchange of ideas is encouraged and equality under law is recognized as the right of every citizen, living in the Deep South will challenge the best minds of our nation. Unusual courage will be required to paddle out of brackish intellectual waters into the mainstream of history.

The magnificent Marten ten Hoor Hall on the University of Alabama campus is indicative of the quest of concerned citizens for excellence. The South needs physical facilities, but it requires also intellectual freedom at its educational institutions. From these halls should go free men who will stop the human loss suffered by the Deep South. For generations, outstanding native sons have migrated to other regions which offered them greater freedom and more opportunity than their own states.

In comparison with Birmingham, Atlanta exemplifies the potential of a relatively free Deep South city. Every year tens of thousands of Georgia's white and Negro agrarians move to Atlanta. Despite this influx, Atlanta's unemployment rate remains below the national average and the city's annual growth in population, economic indicators, and intellectual achievements are envied by other southern urban communities. In contrast, ambitious rural Alabamians by-pass segregated Birmingham, and the city is almost stagnant. Atlanta attracts the brightest members of a rising generation while Birmingham apparently repels them; integration in Atlanta symbolizes a free society, segregation in Birmingham symbolizes a closed one. The contrast between the two cities suggests that freedom in the Deep South could result in retaining its best human resources and attracting desirable people from other states.

To accomplish this reversal in migratory habits, Deep South business and professional men must recognize and assume their responsibilities. To single out ministers is unfair, but by profession they represent the ideal in human relations. Yet when a ministerial association of a Deep South city demands that every public event, football games included, be opened with prayer, but refuses to meet and eat with the Negro ministerial association, thousands of southerners lose their respect for organized religion. The minister who replies with "no comment" to reporters requesting his reaction to the refusal by an usher of his church to seat a Negro and a rector who cancels a religious service on being forewarned of plans to integrate it sear the souls of our brightest young people.

The right of merchant and industrialist to a fair profit is not questioned by American capitalist society. However, those people who define free enterprise in laissez-fair terms, or attempt to make private business of today as sacrosanct as the religious orthodoxy of yesteryear, perpetrate frauds. Unless they locate their enterprises on some unclaimed atoll, the hotel-keeper and restaurant owner of today is subject to numerous regulations. In American cities, owners of private enterprises admit the public nature of their businesses by complying with sanitary and fire ordinances, wage and hour laws, and many other governmental requirements. A national law requiring firms to serve all customers regardless of race would no more strangle free enterprise in the Deep South than state laws similar to it have interfered with private business in a majority of the American states. On the contrary, it would protect the Deep South businessman who welcomes all customers from the predatory tactics of his prejudiced competitor.

To establish a social climate conducive to progress, southerners must disown the "hate Washington" campaign of reactionaries. Individuals working in cooperation with federal and state governments have given our generation its high standard of living. The economies of mass production created big business just as community needs fostered big governments. While the federal government is more powerful today than ever before, so also are state and city governments. Ours is an age of big business and big government.

The Deep South politician who refers to his sovereign state utters nonsense. No politician is so ignorant as to attribute sovereignty to Alabama or Florida or Mississippi for any reason other than to befuddle his listeners. He knows full well that the primacy of the nation has been established by public opinion, war, and court decision. The honest politician who cannot live under the laws of the United States will lead his misguided followers in revolution and suffer the penalties prescribed for treason.

All regions of the nation have resorted to the legitimate doctrine of states' rights to protect peculiar interests. But in the Deep South, states' rights have become synonymous with the desire of a white majority to perpetuate a caste system. Thus a minority within the nation becomes a majority within a state and, while demanding its minority rights, uses its majority status to deny equality under the law to a minority in a state. The use of states' rights to destroy fundamental American principles is not a legitimate exercise of local power.

Evidence of the rabid segregationist's "hate Washington" campaign are billboards which urge the impeachment of Chief Justice Earl Warren. But why stop with Warren? The "separate but equal" issue was under consideration before he became a member of the Court. *Brown* v. *Board of Education* was the unanimous ruling of nine justices and has been unanimously supported by the four members appointed to the Court since 1954. Instead of deserving criticism, the Supreme Court merits commendation for strengthening our basic rights.

The Court also deserves plaudits for another decision which will have far-reaching effects. In the 1960's most Americans possessed two essentials of representative government, universal adult suffrage and free elections. But state legislatures refused to provide equitable reapportionment. By ordering this done, the Supreme Court has given the rapidly increasing urban population of the Deep South the opportunity for a larger role in state and national affairs.

With power and age urbanites may repeal discriminatory acts and insist on fair interpretation of laws. If they do, a minority within a Deep South state will be shorn of its power to undermine an economic program of the majority. Floridians receive a large percentage of their income from the expenditures of tourists. Millions of dollars have been spent to advertise the state's attractiveness, but in 1964 at St. Augustine the use of cattle prods and snarling dogs against people who aspired to first class citizenship did untold damage to the tourist trade. Economists classify this trade as a growth industry, and the Deep South's potential in it is tremendous, but that potential will never be realized as long as racial discrimination exists within its borders.

Southern politicians should consider their role in history as they uphold states' rights for unjust reasons and at the same time boast of their prowess in obtaining federal grants for their constituents. Today's historian studies slavery for two reasons: to condemn it and to examine a historical fact. Tomorrow's historian will study the caste system for two reasons: to condemn it and to examine a historical fact. Yesteryear's coarse, vulgar anti-Negro demagogues have been replaced by suave Deep South politicians who mouth pious words and seek to deny or delay equal citizenship to Negroes. These politicians become gray-haired and distinguished in appearance, follow the prejudiced rabble to win or retain political office, and will win no higher place in history than automatic listing in *Who's Who in America.*

In his essay for a recent book, *We Dissent,* Paul Green declared that "the Old South was an error in history and the Civil War was the horror resulting from that error. . . ." He saw "no salvation to be got now from digging in the sodden dunghill of the Old South and the Civil War. Let's forget them," he advised, "or if we must remember, then remember them for what they were, for their sins and errors, and so keep before us the stern warning of their failures, their perversions, and their death as we work on toward the days of humanity's triumph and a life ahead." These statements came from one who has deep affection for his South.

Critics of this essay may point out omissions, especially those which could have dwelled on the accomplishments of the Deep South and the charm of its people. And they will be on solid ground. With hopeful heart this South Carolinian transplanted in Florida has criticized more than he has praised the land he likes and people he loves. A golden age beckons the Deep South. Every southerner can enter it by supporting basic American principles and perpetuating worthwhile regional tradition.

Comments BY JOHN S. EZELL

Three postulates must be accepted if one is to understand the past and speculate on the future of the Deep South. These are not original premises, but they reinforce the statements of Professor Patrick. While standing alone as characteristics of Southern history, they are also interdependent.

The first is that there presently does not exist an identifiable Deep South, except that it be defined as a state of mind. Its people are not one because of geography, economics, or racial origins (all of which vary widely within any suggested area), but rather because they share common attitudes toward what is viewed by them as common problems. In their eyes, not only are these southern problems, but also they are unique to the South. Part of this common state of mind is a legacy from the past: lessons that they believe themselves to have learned from previously shared experience, both good and bad. For example, the South justified slavery for two centuries on the twin theses that the Negro was biologically inferior, thus incapable of acting like a responsible man, and that he was, therefore, better off in every way under the paternalistic control of the superior white man. Although the South lost the war, nothing occurred that gave southerners a better opinion of the Negro. Even today many southerners view the modern Negro through the stereotype of slavery.

In this common state of mind occur the many myths of southern history, all supported by blind acceptance of a misunderstood past. Here one finds the many myths of Reconstruction, and draws the corollary that, since the one time the Negro enjoyed political equality was also a period of corruption and violence, the Negro has proven himself, therefore, forever incapable of using such rights in a proper manner. To name yet another, here one finds the origins of the myth concerning states' rights. Add to these legacies of the past a siege mentality—the feeling of being surrounded by a hostile world, and its corollary defensive reaction—and one gets the determination to be different and proud of it, even when wrong, that is one of the key characteristics of the Deep South today.

The second postulate is that the pivotal years, 1865 to 1877, in southern history were not and could not be reconstruction years but must be a revolution. Southerners were, and are, unrealistic ever to think there was any possibility of merely rebuilding what the war had destroyed. In the cold absolutes of the period there logically could be no serious thought of replacing the old forms, for their destruction had been one of the primary objectives of the war. "Reconstruction" is a misnomer. There could be nothing less than revolution—economically and socially with the abolition of slavery, and politically with the South surrendering its dominance of the national government for the first time in the nation's history.

At the time too few southerners were willing to see and accept this fact, and this, too, has become a part of the common state of mind today. Yet at no time have there not been some who saw the true lesson of history. For example, even before all the defeated troops had returned home, F. W. Dawson, influential editor of the *Charleston News and Courier,* began to proclaim to any who would listen that the war had taught three things: that slavery had been the cause of all pre-war ills, that the southerner could not live by cotton alone, and that the great significance of the war was that it had emancipated the white man from slavery and cotton. Now was the time for new beginnings. Yet thirty years later, Walter Hines Page, another illustrious son of the South, told a North Carolina audience that three ghosts haunted the South—the Confederate dead, religious orthodoxy, and Negro domination—and that progress would come only when the region had the courage, in his words, "to lift dead men's hands from our life." Failure to wholeheartedly accept this challenge explains much of the bitterness that has characterized this region's history.

The final postulate provides ground for greater optimism. For the reason that change is going to take place whether southerners like it or not, it is important to remember that by the historian's calendar virtually everything, except aspects of the common state of mind, in the South is new. This explains why some southerners are at cross-purposes with other southerners and with the nation as a whole, depending upon the degree to which change has been accepted. The relative newness of the South as we know it today holds out hope for the future. For example, sensitive southerners have long chafed over the relatively low standing of the region educationally when compared with the rest of the nation. These people, and critics of the South, fail to realize that the southern system of public education as we know it today is only about sixty-five years old, with the high school making its appearance only about World War I. Rather than despair over the fact the region has not yet overcome the long lead in time and experience enjoyed by other regions, should not the wonder be that so much has been accomplished in the span of a single life time? In short, many, if not most, of the commonly acknowledged southern deficiencies are the result of lack of time, not inferiority. A final word of caution, however. This should not lead to complacency, but should be a spur to greater endeavors based upon pride in past accomplishments and a new state of mind for the future.

Comments BY ERNEST M. LANDER, JR.

To interpret the history of the Deep South, is to recall a statement by Mr. William Chapman in the *New Republic* of February 20, 1961. "The professional Southerner may fret that he is oppressed, maligned and misunderstood, but he can never complain that he is ignored. The urge, among historians and journalists, to interpret the South and its people is irresistible . . . if Dixie is gone she is not forgotten."

And so it goes. Three or four recent evaluations and interpretations of Southern distinctiveness merit review, especially an article in the October, 1961, *Yale Review,* by David M. Potter. Potter notes that a large number of southern historians, beginning with William E. Dodd, have emphasized Jeffersonianism in the South as the normative: Calhoun and Jefferson Davis were aberrations. These historians contend that Jeffersonianism equals agrarianism equals democracy. In effect, American democracy stemmed primarily from agrarian roots, and these were strong in the South. But Potter asserts that agrarianism implies independence, self-sufficiency, and the hardy yeoman, whereas, actually, in the South commercial, one-crop agriculture with slavery or tenancy has prevailed. The landowners were agricultural businessmen in a money economy. Mr. Potter reminds us that U. B. Phillips saw the South to some extent in these terms, although Phillips concluded that the central theme of southern history is the presence of the Negro.

By contrast, C. Vann Woodward, in his "Search for Southern Identity" in the *Virginia Quarterly Review* (Summer, 1958) attributes Southern distinctiveness to poverty amid national abundance, failure amid national success, a preoccupation with guilt amid the nation's wonderment at its own innocence, slavery in a land which was born free, and the southerner's personal commitment to the concrete and immediate and his fear of abstraction

Potter recognizes a certain validity of these varying interpretations, but he says we need a dissection of the culture. He tentatively suggests that the region is different because of "the culture of the folk," which has survived in the South long after it succumbed to the onslaught of urban-industrial culture elsewhere. In effect, he argues that the relation between the land and the people remained more direct and more primal in the South than in other parts of the country. Even in the most exploitative economic situations the culture retained a personalism in the relations of man to man which industrial society lacks, and a close relationship of man to nature. Hence, is the nostalgia of the South today a yearning, not for agrarianism that did not exist, but for a folk culture that did exist?

Betty E. Chmaj thinks similarly in her attempt to analyze the Radical Right in the South (*Atlantic Monthly*, November, 1962). She finds evidence at every hand of what she calls "paranoid patriotism," where the extreme Rightwingers have simply substituted the abominable Commie for the abominable Yankee. There is among southerners a "naïve conservatism," a "utopian longing to revive the simpler society of a bygone time." At worst this naïve conservatism can produce the Ku Klux Klan, at best, the Nashville Agrarians. Among others who have emphasized the influence of the folk culture are J. M. Dabbs, former president of the Southern Regional Council, and the late Wilbur J. Cash.

But let me concentrate on a more concrete interpretation, one of long standing, U. B. Phillips' "Central Theme of Southern History," the presence of the Negro. This theme has much support among historians and sociologists. Just recently Ralph McGill in his book *The South and the Southerner* stated that the chief southern twig benders were Thomas R. Dew, Benjamin R. Tillman, James K. Vardaman, and Tom Watson, all perhaps best remembered for their racism.

I am in general agreement with Phillips' "Central Theme." In my opinion, there would have been no Civil War without the presence of the Negro here. To be more precise the war was fought not because the Negro was a slave, but because the slave was a Negro—a black man in the midst of a white man's society. To have set him free would have created political, social, and economic problems which the whites simply could not face. As Professor Patrick has noted, even today many southern whites still seem incapable of facing up to the issue charitably or realistically.

After having studied and followed the South's slow and grudging accommodation to federal action in the realm of civil rights, I have concluded that the Deep South, if left to its own devices, would never have abolished slavery. It is inconceivable to me that any ambitious politician would have been rash enough to stand up in the legislative chambers of Mississippi or South Carolina, for example, in 1860, or 1880, or 1900, or 1940, or even

1964 and mildly suggest that perhaps slavery was unjust and that the legislature should begin to consider its abolition.

There is no instance where a state in the Deep South voluntarily and freely granted any significant political right to the Negro race. It has taken a war, constitutional amendments, federal statutes, federal court decisions and injunctions, and even federal marshals and troops to secure for the Negro freedom, political rights, and civil liberties. Yet strangely, when forced to it, most southern whites have accepted these changes in fairly good grace, in South Carolina and Georgia perhaps more so than in Mississippi and Alabama. But, if there is a white person in the Deep South who believes the articulate and educated Negro is satisfied with segregation or even token integration, I can only suggest that he attend an inter-racial meeting of a council on human relations in a southern state. He will quickly be disabused of such a notion. That the old system worked as well as it did was due in large measure to the Negro's character and personality. He seemed ever tractable, forgiving, optimistic about the future; and he retained his sense of humor. Recently a harassed Birmingham Negro college president gave an address in which he warned the whites to read the statistics relative to the black hordes in this world. And he used the phrase "black hordes," though throughout his speech he exhibited a sense of humor and an optimistic outlook. For the most part the Negro leaders recognize the shortcomings of the Negro masses, and they see no great groundswell to the National Association for the Advancement of Colored People, Congress of Racial Equality, and other drives. They continue their demonstrations, no matter how distasteful they may be to the whites, on the old theory that it is the squeaking wheel that gets the grease.

There have been magnificent changes wrought in the southern economy in the past few decades, changes almost incomprehensible to the new generation. Only thirty years ago two-thirds of southern farmers were tenants, earning, according to one study, from $38 to $87 per year per person, and living in homes worth about $350—perhaps $1,000 to $1,200 by today's standards. Malaria and hookworm were common—I know, for as a child

I had both. Running water and electricity were hardly known among rural folk. These figures are within the range of incomes of the poorer, more backward countries of the world today. But thirty years ago a kind of foreign-aid program in Washington began to help the underdeveloped and backward South. Agrarian reform got under way; diversified and more profitable industry moved in; and an economic revolution took place. Dozens of underdeveloped countries in Latin America, Africa, and Asia are trying to accomplish today what the South, in many respects, began just thirty years ago.

Voluminous statistics prove the extent of our great progress and the approach of our standard of living to that of the remainder of the United States. Do not belittle southern achievements, but view them with caution. In 1961 the five Deep South states of South Carolina, Georgia, Alabama, Mississippi, and Louisiana together had fewer bank deposits than either Ohio or Massachusetts, and these same five southern states produced less wealth through manufacturing than did New Jersey. There is still much poverty amidst us. In 1959 52 per cent of all Mississippi families had money income under $3,000. The other four states were slightly better off. Their families with incomes under $3,000 ranged as low as 36 per cent, still a higher percentage than West Virginia, a state that has received much publicity about its poverty-stricken hill people.

Finally, a new study entitled *Racial Crisis in America,* by two Florida State University sociologists soberly reminds us that the problem of race relations is second in gravity only to the threat of nuclear war. The prospect for solution is, at best, one of cold war in the foreseeable future.

Comments BY FRANK FREIDEL

At a recent conference at Rice University on the problems of the South, Professor T. Harry Williams of Louisiana State University commented that what the South requires is less uninformed criticism from without, and more informed criticism from within.

Should someone from outside the Deep South, then, remain silent, be still as southerners discuss the South? Should he feel that he is outside the family and take no part in painful family deliberations? This is not what Professor Williams had in mind, for he referred only to uninformed discussion, and would have been as willing to have abjured uninformed discussion (that is to say, discussion based upon emotion rather than facts) if it took place among southerners themselves. While the historian maturing within the region thereby acquires certain invaluable insights, so also the historian of quite different background can view the South with new perspective. Perhaps the single most important study of the South's most unhappy problem has been the work of a Swede, Gunnar Myrdal's *An American Dilemma.* I would add instantly that it was based largely upon the remarkable advance work of a generation of southern social scientists.

In another sense, outsiders should, and indeed must, participate in discussion of the South, since it is not an isolated island in modern America and the present-day world. Southern problems are American problems which we in the North share and which directly and intimately affect us. As American problems they affect all the people of the United States in their relationships with the rest of the world. Some years ago when I was lecturing abroad I was asked interminably why I was not willing to allow Autherine Lucy to attend the University of Alabama; just last summer, while out of the country, I found myself being held personally responsible for the attitudes and actions of Governors Barnett and Wallace. It was a sobering experience.

It is proper that foreigners should hold me, a northerner, responsible, since in varying degrees the problems of the Deep South have been in the past, and are today, national as well as regional problems. From any point of perspective, similarities as well as differences emerge. It may well be that more studies of a parallel nature are needed. Professor Patrick pointed to the frontier nature of the ante-bellum Deep South; would it not be interesting to compare it more sharply with the western frontier in its institutions and culture? In the same way one might examine the exploitation of the Reconstruction South with that of the territorial west. I agree that the Tweed Ring looted far more successfully than did any plunderers of the South of the same period, and possibly that the territorial carpetbaggers about which Earl Pomeroy has written had better pickings in the Rockies. The South of that era was too poor to be of much profit to anyone within or without.

Other types of comparative studies might also be enlightening. Consider the history of New England where I live: in the Reconstruction era and later, losing out agriculturally to richer areas elsewhere, its textile industry by the twentieth century outmoded and disappearing. This textile industry was dependent until very recently upon competing through advertising with special concessions for new manufacturers and the relatively low pay going to workers, even sending to the vice presidency (and thereby to the White House) a governor whose only positive action was a militantly anti-union statement. And so on.

I have not mentioned white supremacy, nor need I, since every day's newspaper indicates clearly the degree to which this is a national crisis in which we are all involved. Nor have I mentioned urban problems in which the Deep South is rapidly catching up with the North.

Both in the historic past and in the present day we have much in common; we are all in the same family, and we need to counsel together to the best of our ability without mutual animus or pompous sanctimony. In a far larger sense than merely the issue of race relations, the American dilemmas are the dilemmas of all of us. They grow out of the ever-increasing tempo of change in this modern world, in which technology brings innovations so much more rapidly than men emotionally can adjust to them.

Who, other than a handful of fanatics with closed minds, or a minority of hopelessly impractical romantics, can doubt that over-all, regardless of how distasteful to them it has been in part, the changes of the last generation have not been largely for the better? Frightful pockets of poverty still exist in your region and mine, but the total improvement in economic conditions is spectacular. Who would go back to the depression textile wages of about five dollars a week paid both in Greensboro, Georgia, and New Bedford, Massachusetts? Who would go back to an agriculture in which the cash income of innumerable farm families was less than $100 a year?

It is important to remember that the advance of the past thirty years has come, not as an isolated southern phenomenon, but out of a national attack upon the depression, together with the American mobilization during the second World War. The great depression may perhaps have hit the South less hard than the rest of the nation, but if so only because the South had less distance to plummet. By the spring of 1933, when Franklin D. Roosevelt took office and the New Deal began, the Deep South was so desperate that it was ready to accept aid even at the risk of modifying the status quo. Its leaders cherished their states' rights dogma, yet were eager for federal aid. These leaders faced a serious problem because they wanted federal assistance in bringing recovery without the concomitant alteration of existing social and economic institutions. The combination was impossible.

Not that Roosevelt was eager to openly challenge the existing arrangements; there is no evidence that he was other than cautiously neutral. Rather it was that he did not respect the color line in marshaling his attack upon poverty. He wished to improve the lot of all needy Americans regardless of background. Nor could he to any very marked degree fabricate a New Deal especially tailored to southern institutions. His was basically a national program to meet national needs.

Yet the South was near the heart of his thinking. He had spent much time at Warm Springs, Georgia, in his efforts to recuperate from polio, and knew the Deep South intimately and affectionately. He depended heavily upon congressional leaders from the Deep South for the enactment of his program.

In the process, old ways of the Deep South came under attack, and, while the great mass of southerners gave their hearts permanently to Roosevelt, many leaders became uneasy or even hostile. They launched constitutional arguments against the New Deal; they sought refuge against it before the Supreme Court, and for a while they were successful. Roosevelt increasingly aligned himself with those southern leaders in universities, in agriculture and business, and in politics, who were in the forefront of the war on southern poverty, and changes did take place.

The chonges were not entirely the sort that Roosevelt and two of his strong supporters, Senator John H. Bankhead, Jr., and Speaker William B. Bankhead of Alabama, had visualized. The President and the Bankheads were dedicated above all to the rehabilitation of the southern yeoman farmer. Rather profound changes came through wartime industrialization, tapping the resources of the Deep South and employing its skilled labor at good wages. The unskilled or semi-skilled tiller of the soil became more obsolescent than ever.

Once underway, the forces of change have continued. The emphasis has largely changed, but basically the problems are still national ones in which all Americans are involved, and which we might best approach in the spirit of the favorite biblical quotation of our southern President of the United States, "Come, let us reason together."

THE DEEP SOUTH IN TRANSFORMATION

Its Changing Literature

Louis D. Rubin, Jr.

The Literature of a Changing South

It is the custom of those given to writing about the literature of the modern South to see the twentieth century flowering of our region's letters as a unique and unparalleled phenomenon, the sudden coming into being of a great literature, when before there was almost nothing at all. H. L. Mencken, however unintentionally, was the prophet, and the close of the first World War the signal which set the young men of Nashville and Oxford and Chapel Hill to turning out what is beyond doubt the most distinguished body of writing produced in our nation during this century, a literary outburst which effectively gave the lie to the charge that our region was a cultural Gobi.

Now if this is so, and I think it is pretty much so, then the next question is, what caused it to happen? And the question after that, will it continue, and if not, why not?

In order to answer both of these questions, in order better to understand what the questions mean, and what is involved, it will be useful first to get our bearings. I quote, therefore, from a prominent critic and novelist:

> A foreigner studying our current literature, without knowledge of our history, and judging our civilization by our fiction, would undoubtedly conclude that the South was the seat of intellectual empire in America . . .

And from the distinguished president of a southern institution of higher learning:

> Southern literature . . . is not now a name for peculiarities and sentimental gush, but it stands for a fresh, first-hand, brave, liberal treatment of life and nature, past and present, in the South.

And from a noted critic and scholar:

> more men and women are writing fiction, poetry, plays, and literary criticism than at any time in the past quarter of a century, and . . . they are displaying a critical intelligence, a sense of literary values, and a reaction against sentimentalism and romance which has not been hitherto regarded as characteristic of Southern writing.

And from a study of a group of southern writers:

> the work of the writers of the . . . South must inevitably constitute a long and distinguished chapter in the history of Southern letters, one absolutely essential to the understanding of that history.

The first of these quotations is from the novelist and Reconstruction politician Albion Tourgée, and was written in 1888. The second is from Henry Nelson Snyder, writing in the *South Atlantic Quarterly* in 1902. The third is from Edwin Mims's *The Advancing South,* published in 1926. The last is from an introduction to a book about modern southern literature published last fall, and written by myself.

The point is that there is nothing particularly new to the notion that southern literature is undergoing a momentous flowering. It was said in the 1870s and 1880s about Sidney Lanier, Irwin Russell, George Washington Cable, Augusta Evans Wilson, Sherwood Bonner, Joel Chandler Harris, and Margaret Junkin Preston. I suspect, though a hasty search did not turn up a quotation that said so in just so many words, that the same was being said in the decade before the Civil War about William Gilmore Simms, Paul Hamilton

Hayne, Philip Pendleton, John Esten Cooke, George W. Bagby, Henry Timrod, John R. Thompson, John Pendleton Kennedy, Thomas Holley Chivers, and Edgar Allan Poe. Certainly in the early 1900s it was said of James Lane Allen, Samuel Minturn Peck, Mary Noailles Murfree, Grace Elizabeth King, Cale Young Rice, Lizette Reese, Thomas Nelson Page, O. Henry, and Mrs. Burton Harrison. Just after World War I it was being said about Irvin S. Cobb, Ellen Glasgow, James Branch Cabell, William Alexander Percy, Corra Harris, Julia Peterkin, Frances Newman, and Du Bose Heyward. In the 1930s it was said, and is still being said, of William Faulkner, Thomas Wolfe, Robert Penn Warren, Allen Tate, John Crowe Ransom, Donald Davidson, Erskine Caldwell, Andrew Lytle, T. S. Stribling, Katherine Anne Porter, Lillian Hellman, Stark Young, and Elizabeth Madox Roberts. Now we talk of William Styron, Flannery O'Connor, Eudora Welty, Carson McCullers, Peter Taylor, James Agee, Tennessee Williams, Randall Jarrell, James Dickey, Walter Sullivan, George Garrett, Shelby Foote, Reynolds Price, Truman Capote, Shirley Ann Grau, and Madison Jones.

It is, in other words, an old southern custom. We have always had a goodly supply of writers, and we have always bragged on them. In the early years of this century a group of editors and book promoters could publish and sell thousands of copies of a seventeen-volume set of books, thick and gilded, entitled *The Library of Southern Literature,* containing selections from the work of many dozens of southern authors, most of whom we can scarcely remember today. What would be the size of a similar collection published now? It is enough to stagger the imagination.

I mention all this not in order to suggest that those writers whom we now consider among the leading American authors—Faulkner, Wolfe, Warren, Ransom, Tate, Porter,

Welty, Styron, Jarrell, a few others—are the beneficiaries, or perhaps the victims, of being somewhat over-praised, for I do not think they are. The estimate we place on them is shared throughout the nation and on several continents. We do not need our own critics and journalists to say it for us. Southern literature is a matter of international interest.

It is probable, of course, that time will winnow the harvest, just as it has blurred the Simmses, Haynes, Laniers, Harrisons, Pages, Thompsons, Glasgows, Cobbs, Striblings, and Robertses, and we shall perhaps be left with Poe, Twain (whom we did not claim as our own during his lifetime, though surely he is that), Faulkner, Wolfe, Ransom, and one or two others. No one can tell about such things. The vanity of literary estimate and the ephemerality of literary fashion are no new phenomena. Still, one recalls these pathetically brave words of Byron, writing in opposition to the Lake Poets:

> Scott, Rogers, Campbell, Moore, and Crabbe, will try
> 'Gainst you the question with posterity.

It is a two-edged sword, because despite Byronic satire, Wordsworth and Coleridge have proved to be just as enduring as poets as their contemporary admirers thought them, and if Byron was right about Southey, he was wrong about those he would have substituted in their place. Indeed, contemporary estimates are quite as likely to be right as to be wrong, if not more likely to be.

But to return to the South: the question to be asked is this. If each generation of southerner has produced its poets and novelists, then why has it turned out that, with one or two exceptions, only that generation of southern writers who came into prominence in the late 1920s and the 1930s seems to have produced a body of literature of really major stature? What happened to the South so that the same region, the same people, should suddenly have developed not merely good writers, but great writers, literary figures of worldwide importance, whose best words show little sign of diminishing in reputation or readership? And what does that mean for the present generation of southern writers, those who must follow this distinguished group?

The answer to the why of it is not exactly new. That delightfully enthusiastic literary scholar C. Alphonso Smith suggested it as long ago as 1908, though he was a bit premature in his evaluation of the evidence, when he saw southern literature as being the product of a period of great social change. Smith pointed to Elizabethan England, when, he said, England became a manufacturing country and promptly produced Shakespeare and his contemporaries. He pointed to the England of the Napoleonic War period, when the steam engine was revolutionizing British commerce and industry, and saw Wordsworth, Coleridge, Keats, Shelley, Byron, Scott, Burns, and Burke as the result. He pointed to the period from 1830 to 1845 in England, when railroads, steamship travel, and the telegraph revolutionized British trade, and there resulted Tennyson, the Brownings, Dickens, Thackeray, Eliot, Ruskin, and Carlyle.

It is obvious, Smith declared, that "great literary movements are the expression of national awakenings. They presuppose a quickening of the national life and a broadening of the national outlook. They imply the presence of some mighty influence that brings about a community of interest and effort together with the emancipation of hope and vision. . . . Literary productiveness, in other words, is vitally related to industrial productiveness, both being correlative manifestations of the creative spirit."

Smith then proceeded to explain the achievement in southern literature since the Reconstruction by the awakening caused by the impact of industrialization on the region. There were, in other words, no southern writers of much importance until the New South of Henry W. Grady and his friends came into being. The words of Sidney Lanier in 1870 he found prophetic: "Day by day . . . a thousand vital elements rill through my soul. Day by day the secret deep forces gather, which will presently display themselves in bending leaf and waxy petal and in useful fruit and grain."

C. Alphonso Smith was a product of the ideology of the New South. Like Grady, Walter Hines Page, Edwin A. Alderman, and others, he felt that industrialism would cure the regional ills. But that generation of southern writers who came after Smith (and it is pertinent to remember Smith died in 1924), and who did in fact seem to have attained the kind of momentous cultural awakening that Smith thought he had seen in Lanier, Maurice Thompson, Joel Chandler Harris, Mary Noailles Murfree, James Lane Allen, George W. Cable, and Thomas Nelson Page, can hardly be said to have written in praise of factory smoke. Faulkner's modern-day South is in his best novels the wasteland of T. S. Eliot in a rural setting, and it is inhabited by the likes of Flem Snopes, Jason Compson, and Percy Grimm. Warren scarcely can be said to have constructed Willie Stark and Hogan Murdock along complimentary lines. Altamont in Old Catawba is not a pretty town. The response of the Nashville writers to the factories is well known. And so on; if poets are indeed supposed to have a vested interest in human misery, then the southern branch of the tribe has found rich dividends in the modern industrial South.

The truth seems to be that Professor Smith was quite correct in detecting a causal relationship between industrialization and literary productivity, but in interpreting the relationship simply in terms of an awakening being accompanied by or causing another awakening, he was examining the evidence superficially. For if relationship there is, it has to do not so much with the kind of easy optimistic enthusiasm that Professor Smith thought was at work as with something much more profound. It has to do with social change. It is what can happen if a society which has one kind of identity and one kind of texture of values, attitudes, beliefs, customs, and assumptions that constitute its social and moral fabric is suddenly confronted with great changes in its ways of doing things. This is not primarily a matter of economics, though it perhaps arises out of economic change. Rather, it is a change in the basic premises under which a society functions. It is a modification that involves religious ideals, moral values, social structure, historical memories, blood ties of kith and kin, political loyalties, aesthetic inclinations. Any society is predicated upon such values and attitudes, which together define its image of the good life, its worthy ideals and standards. But these values and attitudes never exist in an abstract form; they are rooted in institutions. When, therefore, the institutions, the texture of the daily life, are dramatically changed, the result is dislocation and confusion while the society proceeds to explore what the changes mean for it. Old and accustomed attitudes have to be reshaped to new demands and new conditions. Such was indeed the Elizabethan Age in England, and the Romantic period as well; and also the New England Renaissance in our own country before the Civil War, and the Irish literary revival just before and after the turn of the century, and the great period of the Russian novel before that. And surely this is true of our Southland in the twentieth century.

It is true because the very nature of literature is concerned with such things. For literature is above all an ordering process; the writer gives form to life, and thus his experience is made meaningful. Often this is understood too narrowly. Thus when a writer fails to choose for his subject matter the immediate events of his society's day-by-day existence, and writes instead of kings in Denmark, and man's disobedience to man, and the pursuit of a white whale, and a governess of an English estate, and the playing of a sonata at a Parisian salon, and drifting down the Mississippi on a raft, and knight errants riding forth to do battle with knaves, he is pronounced to be unconcerned with the life going on around him, and his books are declared as of little or no value in understanding that life. But writers are not necessarily journalists, and they ought not to be expected to perform that function. They are concerned with the human condition, and in their stories and poems they seek to give order to human experience through form. They are interested in what it means to be a human being, and in creating an image of human life they are attempting to reconcile what is always the apparent contradiction in ideals and values on the one hand and the nature of actual existence on the other.

Allen Tate, in an oft-quoted statement, has declared that the southern writer of his generation was, by virtue of his time and place, unable to view his experience with an historical perspective that came from the conditions of twentieth century southern experience. He referred to a "looking two ways" whereby the post-World War I southern poet or novelist observed modernity through the eyes of the past, and also viewed his cultural and social tradition from the vantage point of one who could no longer assume its premises without questioning them. It provided him and his fellow southern authors, "at any rate in Nashville," with a "double focus," which "gave a special dimension to the writings of our school. . . ." In another essay Mr. Tate detected approximately the same kind of experience in the work of the New England poet Emily Dickinson, who, he said, "was born into the equilibrium of an old and a new order," one which provided "the perfect literary attention."

So the answer I propose to my first question, which had to do with why the generation of southern writers of the 1920s and 1930s did indeed produce a body of literature of the utmost importance, is that they did so because they grew up and acquired their experience at a time when the life of which they were part provided in a most dramatic fashion the image of man seeking to define himself, a time of tension between values and circumstances when men were both changing and resisting change. Their compulsion was—and I am reminded of Thomas Mann's remark that genius is not a gift but a compulsion—to seek to discover form and order in that experience, and their novels, stories and poems constitute what they discovered.

It has been said, for example, that William Faulkner is almost the single American writer of our century whose work is of genuinely tragic stature. If this is so, then we need only ask ourselves what tragedy is, in order to grasp its relevance to his time and place. For when Aristotle speaks of tragedy as being "an imitation of an action that is serious, complete, and of a certain magnitude," and when he insists that the tragic poet must "prefer probable impossibilities to improbable possibilities," he is only insisting that a tragedy is a meaningful ordering of experience. Within apparent disorder and violence the tragic poet discovers moral meaning; out of the confusion and turbulence attendant on the change of southern society from one thing into another, the novelist, if he is a Faulkner, achieves the moral ordering of tragedy. (Be it noted that Aristotle himself remarks the change of fortune necessary to tragedy.)

It was the changing South that helped to make possible the high attainment of southern writing in the years between the two world wars. Now I come, however belatedly, to the next question, which is whether those conditions are still operative, and if they are not, why they are no longer so. What are the chances for a continuing twentieth century renaissance in southern literature? Or to put it more specifically, Faulkner and Wolfe are dead. Warren, Ransom, Tate, and most of the others are in their sixties and their seventies. What of their successors? What may we legitimately expect of the literary generation which has come into prominence since the end of World War II?

At first glance the answer to my question may appear pleasingly obvious, if my premises as to what caused the southern literary renascence are accepted. I say pleasingly—I speak as a literary critic when I do, and not as a citizen of our region. For surely there is no need to demonstrate in the year 1964 that there is still a great deal of turbulence and disorder involved in the South's transition from one kind of society to another. Alabama is right in the middle of it, especially as regarding one key problem and image of that change. The Negro has been the symbol of the whole transaction; a study of the southern literary image of the Negro as it has changed over the past century, from Uncle Remus to Joe Christmas, would be tantamount to a moral history of the southern states. Yet far more than civil rights is involved in this business. The change has been of greater scope than that; it has pervaded almost every aspect of our society. I think of something that occurred to me the other day. I was in the barber shop getting a haircut, and was chatting with the barber about television programs. The barber is a man of about sixty, who was raised on a farm in the western Virginia mountains. He was telling me about a program he especially enjoyed on Friday nights. It is called "That Was The Week That Was." Now without venturing into television criticism, I might comment that the program in question, whatever its comic merits, is a highly sophisticated affair as television programs go, and the kind of experience it deals with and reflects is a long way removed from that of someone growing up in the 1900s on a mountain farm in Virginia. Yet this man, who like others of his profession, is not a person of extraordinary intellectual gifts, could find much enjoyment, and presumably some meaning, in the program. And to the extent that my barber is in any way representative of his fellow citizenry, what does this suggest about what has happened to our once somnolent, settled, contained, predominantly agricultural and rural region during this century?

It suggests—and of course we have far more verifiable evidence than my barber in Roanoke upon which to base conclusions about it—that our society is not only undergoing great change, but that it has been doing so for some time now. The fact is that we are confronted with a society and a culture of towns and cities, not of farms and villages. The dominant mode of southern life, both statistically and, more important still, in spirit and attitude, is much more urban, and much less rural, than it used to be not so many years ago. And this is bound to have its impact on our writers.

Look at it this way. William Faulkner grew up in a small town. So did Robert Penn Warren, Allen Tate, John Crowe Ransom, Donald Davidson, Andrew Lytle, Stark Young, Katherine Anne Porter, Elizabeth Madox Roberts. Asheville, North Carolina, when Thomas Wolfe was born there was a town of some 14,000 population. What of the leading post-World War II southern writers? William Styron grew up in the shipbuilding city of Newport News, Virginia. Randall Jarrell and Walter Sullivan are from Nashville, and Peter Taylor from Memphis, Tennessee. James Dickey grew up in Atlanta. Flannery O'Connor is a native of Savannah, Georgia. Eudora Welty is from Jackson, Mississippi, James Agee from Knoxville, Tennessee, Carson McCullers from Columbus, Georgia, and Truman Capote and Shirley Ann Grau were both born in New Orleans. What, in short, has happened to that predominantly rural experience? And even the small town is not the isolated farming community it used to be, what with modern mass communications, four-lane highways, and the like. In this respect as in others the South has changed; the recent political troubles over legislative reapportionment are but one sign of it. My barber in Roanoke is another.

What I am trying to suggest is that this is the change that is most important for the South, and not topical problems such as civil rights. Indeed, the developments in civil rights during the decade since *Brown* v. *Board of Education* could only have been possible because the other change has taken place. It is, if I may say so, predominantly an urban development; it would never have taken place if the South's Negro population had remained primarily on the farms.

Now what does this mean for the southern writer? It means that his experience must by its very nature be vastly different in many important respects from that of his predecessors. And since the experience of his predecessors involved the transition from the rural and traditional to the urban and cosmopolitan society rather than his own experience, since it is the result of just the kind of experience that helped to form the art of his predecessors, it is not going to be that of his predecessors. In a sense, he is beginning where they left off; he is starting out from the city, not traveling from rural countryside to city. And if we may use "urban experience" and "industrialism" as being in important ways synonymous, then we can say that the experience of the current generation is much more that of full-fledged participation in an industrial society than that of the previous generation.

Social change, to repeat, means reinterpretation and revision of religious ideals, moral values, political loyalties; for the southern writer it opened up for scrutiny his tradition, his history, his social attitudes, his religious assumptions, his moral, ethical, and esthetic promises. It forced him to redefine himself, and he did so in his poems and stories. Does this change in attitude mean, then, that despite the experience of transition that the previous generation found so momentously fruitful, the younger southern writer cannot partake of what Allen Tate said was the "perfect literary situation," that of being born into "an equilibrium of the old and the new order"? And will Tate's prediction for southern writing, expressed elsewhere, that "the focus of this consciousness," "the curious burst of intelligence that we get at a crossing of the ways," is "quite temporary," be likely to prove correct?

One does not like to think so. And, indeed, it would seem highly premature to say such a thing. For surely this process of transition involves more than actual geographical displacement. Surely the process of adjusting to new experience, of learning how to square old ideals, attitudes, and values with their embodiment in new and different circumstances and institutions is still far from being over. It would hardly be accurate to declare that the South has by now mastered and assimilated its urban experience, and that the travail of transition is no longer taking place within our minds and hearts. Everything we know and read and see would indicate otherwise. So if literary achievement thrives on the problems of definition involved in the turmoil of social change, there is still plenty of it left for the younger writers.

One therefore, finally, refuses to predict. And so I choose to end my discourse with a few additional generalizations, having to do, not with what is possible for us, but what would seem to me to be necessary if we are to use our opportunities.

My first generalization has to do with the use of our literary heritage. What the southern writer of the present generation must do, if he is to give his poems and stories the stature and range of important literature, is to write out of his own experience, and not that of his immediate predecessors, no matter how great. He must, in short, learn what can be used, and what must be discarded, if he is to be himself. One of the difficulties of following along after great writers is that the force of their own vision is so powerful, so pervasive, that it exercises a spell over those who read it. But literature is the act of discovering meaning through language and form. And unless that spell is broken, and unless it is prevented from dominating the modes of discourse and habits of perception of the younger writer, he will to that extent be hindered from discovering the meaning of his own experience, which in important respects is different from the experience of the previous generation.

My second generalization is that critical and reading taste always lags behind artistic insight. The vogue of southern writing in our time has been such that it is temptingly easy for the young writer to seek to work squarely within that vogue, with the relatively easy prospect of immediate success, financial as well as critical, available to anyone who seems to meet the demand for a continuation of what is now known and familiar. Yet the only literature ultimately worth writing is the literature which focuses squarely and clearly with absolute honesty upon what the writer can really discover about human experience, not on what he is told that he should be discovering by book reviewers and by semi-annual royalty statements.

My last generalization is that during the past half-century the South has changed a great deal. It has given up many old ideas and has accepted many new ideas, and it has surrendered many tenaciously-held attitudes and habits and has accepted many new ones. At the same time it has refused to give up some of its old ideas, and to change some of its traditional attitudes and habits. Much of what the South has given up we are well rid of; much of what we have acquired we can put to very good use. Some of what we have retained we probably ought not to retain; some of what we have not accepted we would do well to keep right on refusing to accept. And lastly, we have given up some things we should never have relinquished, and we have welcomed some things we ought to have spurned. This is always the way with change; and doubtless it will always be. But there is one southern institution we cannot afford ever to relinquish, and which we must hold onto, no matter what comes. Faulkner called it "love and honor and pity and pride and compassion and sacrifice." Allen Tate called it "knowledge carried to the heart." Robert Penn Warren called it "the awful responsibility of Time." Whatever it is called, it is the old human impulse to look deeply and honestly at what we are, never to deny what we must be, never to settle for less than what we might become, and always to seek to understand and cherish our experience. Another name for this, in our own time, has been William Faulkner.

Comments BY CARL BENSON

A major factor in the changing literature of the South, frequently asserted, is the importance of a divided society and economy. In such a society, in the midst of shifting values, impulses, even conditions, develop the sensitive awareness and exacerbated conscience without which, probably, there can be no major art. Although Mr. Rubin clearly is pointing to a major factor in his assertions, it cannot be said that there is any necessary relationship here. To claim definitively cause-and-effect would involve dangerous and specious scientism. It is true, as many have pointed out, that the South has been the only part of the country that has had the tragic experience of losing a war. If the early literary reflections of this lost cause were the sentimentalities of Thomas Nelson Page (and the sentimental continues to appeal, as witness Margaret Mitchell), the same lost cause continued to reverberate until it formed a part of the brooding philosophy of a Faulkner or a Warren. With the awareness of the meaning of defeat must be associated the failure of a system based on slavery, a variety of accumulated exasperations and guilts; and all these together must, for the sensitive mind, raise questions of the significance of the past and of capacity for responsibility. C. Vann Woodward illustrates some of the extensions:

> An age-long experience with human bondage and its evils and later with emancipation and its shortcomings did not dispose the South very favorably toward such popular American ideas as the doctrine of human perfectibility, the belief that every evil has a cure, and the notion that every human problem has a solution. For these reasons the utopian schemes and the gospel of progress that flourished above the Mason and Dixon line never found very wide acceptance below the Potomac during the nineteenth century. In that most optimistic of centuries in the most optimistic part of the world, the South remained basically pessimistic in its social outlook and its moral philosophy. The experience of evil and the experience of tragedy are parts of the Southern heritage that are as difficult to reconcile with the American legend of innocence and social felicity as the experience of poverty and defeat are to reconcile with the legends of abundance and success.*

While no one can avoid acknowledging the impact of such conditions as Woodward describes upon the writers of a region, perhaps we ought to remember the obvious, that a period of great writing is a lucky accident, the mysterious and incalculable occurrence of genius. To refer to one of Mr. Rubin's examples, the brutal autonomy of the Tsars in the nineteenth century finally oppressed the little people so much that the spirit of rebellion was in the very air. Chekhov and Turgenev spoke of individual human freedoms delicately and directly. At the same time Dostoievsky explored ranges of individual guilt and redemption, and Tolstoy, with the problem posed largely by the collision of Mother Russia with Napoleon, was off muttering

* *The Burden of Southern History* (Baton Rouge: Louisiana State University Press, 1960), p. 21.

grandly on historical causality. Although Russian conditions, in addition to a variety of winds from the West, constituted a necessary matrix, it is still a piece of phenomenal luck that four such indisputable geniuses should be writing at the same time. It may be suggested, too, that the lucky accidents of Faulkner and Warren peculiarly enrich the southern renaissance, and, if it were not for them, its luster would be considerably diminished.

And this leads to a point of emphasis which might be different from Mr. Rubin's. Sometimes he seems in danger of throwing a loving lasso around all southern writers, claiming a group of virtues for the writers as a group. Such a practice blurs significant distinctions, some of which have been suggested by the writers themselves. Warren, for example, does not share Mr. Rubin's high regard for Wolfe. Though he admires some of Wolfe's characters, especially in *Look Homeward Angel,* he obviously regards Wolfe's talent as largely dissipated by a wanton egocentricity. When Faulkner is probing the depths of tragedy, the plight of the characters looms so large that the fact that they are southerners seems only secondary. *Absalom, Absalom!* moves through southern history (a history, incidentally, vastly different from that of Davidson or Tate); but Sutpen, the tragic protagonist, is guilty of an inhumane materialism, which, ranging through all levels of what should be human communion, damns him to his destiny. Faulkner sees materialism as the curse of America, not simply of the South. One might reasonably reverse the field and argue that when "southernness" becomes obsessive, as it does frequently in Mr. Davidson, it has effects that must be regarded as serious flaws. Only the symbolic, almost mythopoeic figure of Lee sustains "Lee in the Mountains." "The Tall Men" is almost ruined by Agrarian polemical impurities, as *The Grapes of Wrath* is almost ruined by the impurities of social theory, and as the Catholic novels of Graham Greene are seriously hurt by religious propaganda. There are, to be sure, different degrees of southern obtrusiveness. In his fine and carefully articulated novel, *The Velvet Horn,* Lytle magically juggles a fantastic number of symbolic, even allegorical, effects and points of view. He gives us the Garden, symbolic withdrawal from a contemporary world, a young man's initiation into selfhood, incest that is not simply factual but symbolic. All in all, it is a very complicated and suggestive novel; because it is, Lytle could have spared us some of his indulging in southern talk, especially on the part of Uncle Jack; the talk does impede our understanding of a distinguished novel that already has enough hurdles.

Subsequent readers may reverse my judgments, but there is a point to make: we have already had enough criticism of southern writers, especially the Fugitive-Agrarians, as a group. I would like to see future critics separate them and make discriminating evaluations of them individually. Faulkner, the one generally acknowledged great writer of the modern South, is frequently lumped, for example, with weaker talents for the purpose of shoring them up a bit. Here is a part of a sentence from Allen Tate: "Two other writers of prose-fiction, Mr. Stark Young and Miss Eudora Welty, quite as gifted as Mr. Faulkner, if somewhat below him in magnitude and power. . . ."* There is little sense of claiming equality of gift on the one hand while denying equality of magnitude and power on the other.

Just as Faulkner is outside the net of the Agrarians, for a variety of reasons, but chiefly because of his profounder tragic insight and because his convictions about the curse of slavery do not at all jibe with the presuppositions of an Agrarian squirearchy, so would I question the wisdom of calling Mark Twain a southerner. The southern writers with whom Twain had a great affinity were perhaps J. G. Baldwin, J. J. Hooper, and the like; but these were, though southern in scene, frontier humorists. It was in this capacity that they became Twain's teachers. Faulkner afterwards went to school to them all, of course, but this fact does not give the South any especial claim on all-American Twain.

In at least one other way we must beware of claiming too much for the South. There is the complex question of literary heritage. After all, there lurks behind Faulkner's capacity to con-

* "A Southern Mode of the Imagination," *Carleton Miscellany*, Winter, 1960, 9.

front the world as tragic more than simply southern consciousness of the divided heart, more than just the will to create a fictional order in answerable style. Faulkner learned part of his aims and craft from Balzac, Dickens, and Conrad; and the King James Version of the Bible resounds through his works as well as the wildly humorous, yet bitterly ironic range of Twain. Ransom's poems are characterized by southern gentility, but it is a gentility that has been modified by an admiration for Donne and a certain distrust for Aristotle.

If I am not so sanguine as Mr. Rubin, however, let us recognize that the South since 1920 has made the nation's greatest contribution in great and near-great writers. Most of the names Rubin has mentioned are worthy of serious attention. It may be as the present older generation passes from the scene, as the Civil War and Reconstruction drift further from us out of the memory of the last grandson, as the South embraces more and more the urbanization that accompanies industry, that some cherished southern inflections will disappear from all but deliberately historical fiction. Specifically southern rural scenes may become less common, and we can do without whimsical blue-nosed colonels, or a repetition of Stark Young's sentiments, however charming they may have been at first. The southern country that may continue to matter will be, in part at least, the country of the mind in the sense of which Flannery O'Connor speaks:

> When we talk about the writer's country we are liable to forget that no matter what particular country it is, it is inside as well as outside him. Art requires a delicate adjustment of the outer and inner worlds in such a way that, without changing their nature, they can be seen through each other. To know oneself is to know one's region. It is also to know the world, and it is also, paradoxically, a form of exile from that world.*

Though regional conventions, social patterns, and particular commitments may change, man's need for formulations of his essential quests will continue to take place in both inner and outer

* "The Fiction Writer and His Country," in Granville Hicks (ed.), *The Living Novel* (New York: Macmillan, 1957), p. 163.

countries, and the seriously daring writer will write out of the conditions that are fated for him.

The future for southern letters is bright simply because great writing begets great writing. The great Russians of the nineteenth century challenged one another; we can see this in Gorky's sensitive little book, *Reminiscences of Tolstoy, Chekhov, and Andreyev*. Similarly, Faulkner is still with us to excite admiration and emulation in young writers. The same can be said of Katherine Anne Porter, Warren, Ransom, and the others. Of course, the simple copier of devices will not amount to much, and limited regionalist will pay the proper price of limited appeal. But the massive models are there for those young writers who will seriously enter the contest with all the craft they can bring to bear in their search for truths about the eternally divided human condition.

Comments BY HUDSON STRODE

In the 1890's Gordon Coogler, a minor South Carolina poet, made a famous statement: "Alas, for the South; her books have grown fewer. She never was much given to literature." His statement about the fewer books was indeed true. Southerners were too shattered by the War Between the States and Reconstruction to indulge in creative writing. Up to this twentieth century the South had produced only a slim handful of first rate literary men: Poe, Mark Twain, Sidney Lanier; and, great in a minor field, Joel Chandler Harris; and in a lesser sense, Thomas Nelson Page, George Washington Cable, and O. Henry. There were other writers, some quite popular, like Augusta Evans Wilson, but they hardly produced literature.

So Henry Mencken was not exaggerating much when he shocked and infuriated the South in 1920 with his famous essay "The Sahara of the Bozart," in which he declared there was no first-rate writer south of Richmond's Ellen Glasgow and James Branch Cabell.

Mencken, some may remember, was burned in effigy by outraged Mississippians. And Mississippi shortly became the most talented state in the Union. Think of Stark Young, perhaps the finest dramatic critic this country has produced; William Faulkner, Nobel Prize winner; Eudora Welty, Elizabeth Spencer, William Alexander Percy, Walter Percy, Ben Ames Williams, Shelby Foote, Thomas Hal Phillips, Borden Deal, Hodding Carter, Ellen Douglas, just to name a few of them.

Golden veins of talent were tapped, and the whole South became productive in a truly amazing way. Why? How came this burst of literary achievement? Louis Rubin has given you some good answers. I shall give you another—a somewhat humorous one. Frances Newman, that brilliant, acid critic and Atlanta librarian, author of *The Hard Boiled Virgin* and a pet of Mencken and Cabell, had an original explanation. She once said to me in her dripping-sweet Georgia accent: "Why, it just had never occurred to us that the North expected us Southerners to *write* books—we only read them. But as soon as Mr. Mencken told us what was expected of us, of course, we started writing from the Atlantic Seaboard to the plains of West Texas."

In any case, Mencken really blasted the South out of its literary apathy, and the next three decades—the thirties, the forties, and the fifties—became the first golden age of southern literature. One has only to recall the top man of letters, William Faulkner, and the top woman of letters, Katherine Anne Porter, and Thomas Wolfe and Erskine Caldwell. Caldwell's *Tobacco Road* and *God's Little Acre,* ribald, realistic novels of poor white southern life, published in 1932 and 1933 respectively, became world best sellers.

In 1936 came Margaret Mitchell's *Gone With the Wind,* which also made global fame. For vitality of character and dramatic excitement of its kind it will perhaps never be surpassed.

During the decade of the 1940's Carson McCullers from Columbus, Georgia, burst forth at twenty-three with *The Heart Is a Lonely Hunter* to win praise from American critics, and later, from eminent foreign commentators.

And in 1945 and 1947, with *The Glass Menagerie* and *A Streetcar Named Desire,* Tennessee Williams, a native of Columbus,

Mississippi, became America's foremost playwright after Eugene O'Neill.

Not long after Mencken's blast, emerged three great writers of Negro novels: Du Bose Heyward with *Porgy,* Julia Peterkin with *Black April* and *Scarlet Sister Mary,* which won a Pulitzer Prize, and Roark Bradford whose novel became the play, *The Green Pastures.*

With his powerful novel *Native Son* Richard Wright from the Mississippi Delta proved to be the number one Negro prose writer in America until James Baldwin came along.

After 1930 it became a most usual thing for southern writers to win Pulitzer Prizes, among them, Margaret Mitchell, Julia Peterkin, Marjorie Kinnan Rawlings, Elizabeth Madox Roberts, Ellen Glasgow, A. B. Guthrie, Jr., Douglas Southall Freeman, Paul Green, Jesse Stuart, T. S. Stribling, John Gould Fletcher, and Robert Penn Warren. In 1962 Alabama's Harper Lee won the Pulitzer Prize with *To Kill a Mockingbird.* William Faulkner, who already had a Nobel Prize, won a second Pulitzer in 1963 with *The Reivers.* And John Crowe Ransom was awarded the Pulitzer Prize for poetry in 1964.

The variety of talent in the South may be exemplified by Alabama's William March, who, in *Company K,* produced perhaps the best novel of World War I, and Tennessee's James Agee, with his evocative, sensitive *A Death in the Family.*

Today the South can boast of contemporary Truman Capote, Eudora Welty, William Styron, Reynolds Price, as well as Katherine Anne Porter and Carson McCullers. There are also Flannery O'Connor, Elizabeth Spencer, Harriet Arnow, Jesse Stuart, Andrew Lytle, Calder Willingham, Peter Fiebelman, Shirley Ann Grau, Borden and Babs Deal, Lonnie Coleman, Elise Sanguinetti, Cecil Dawkins and Harper Lee.

So the cultural map of the South, with its new symphony orchestras, its art museums, and its distinguished writers has undergone a mighty metamorphosis since 1920. Instead of the literary desert Henry Mencken beheld, the scene has changed to a wide-spread flowering oasis, albeit its palm trees sometimes bear bitter fruit.

The point in question now is whether the present-day southern literature is becoming less southern. The answer is, I think, no. It is still definitely southern, but written from a more modern viewpoint. Many of the old themes and materials that made it exciting have been done to death.

The Gothic School of southern literature, which Faulkner carried to its greatest expression, has passed. Anyone writing today about the decayed old plantation house, the endlessly involved family connections, the tragic story often full of horror and the comedy sometimes grotesquely farcical, might incur the charge of repetition.

The note today is less aristocratic, less on faded gentility, and much more plebeian. Witness Harper Lee's small town middle-class and Reynolds Price's country folk. Novelists of tomorrow will doubtless leave out most of the magnolias, the wisteria and the white columns, as well as the lynchings, the rapes, the half-wits, the degenerates, and the degrading poverty of *Tobacco Road*. However, there will still be skeletons in closets to be revealed and made use of dramatically by talents like those of Tennessee Williams and Lillian Hellman.

When, in 1944, Georgia's Lillian Smith made a sensational hit with a novel of miscegenation, *Strange Fruit*, which ended in a dramatic lynching, it marked the end of lynching as a good workable theme in southern letters. Lynching as a major theme is done with; it is certainly stale now, no matter who employs it.

With the economic improvement in the South under Franklin Roosevelt, the material that helped to make Erskine Caldwell outstanding has to a large extent disappeared. Good roads, rural school buses, old age pensions, social security, and various government handouts, like free food, have banished from real life and the stage the vivid Jeeter Lesters. The poverty-stricken of, say, *Grapes of Wrath* will no longer be used effectively, unless one writes of the misery in the Kentucky coal mining regions. Even Faulkner's Snopses have to a degree become more respectable today and have lost some part of the redness of their necks.

The trend seems to point away from the rural scene to the

industrial urban. Yet, with the new power and the richer emoluments of labor, the day of the so-called "proletarian" novel, as such, is done with.

Books dealing with the charming, inimitable, old-fashioned Negroes, who understand and appreciate what is called "quality folk," and still speak in warm, mellow accents, will doubtless disappear completely. But the Negro in his new political and economic status and his determined struggle for equality will furnish material for some forthcoming novels. The dearth of house servants has made depleting inroads on the proverbial southern hospitality, and consequently affects the tone of southern fiction.

As democracy spreads its leveling processes, much of the flavor and the striking contrasts that made southern literature colorful will vanish. But climate will always make a difference. Northerners and mid-westerners who come to live among us generally soften their r's as the years pass and succumb to the slower southern rhythms. Though air conditioning has made a blessed difference inside our houses, so far the climate outside remains the same. Few can resist for long the over-all softness of the southern climate. Strangers who abide with us will in the end be influenced by the long hot summers and the occasional beguiling spring days in the midst of winter.

Those southern natives who move to New York, like Capote and McCullers, Williams and Hellman, never escape from the South's subtle influence. With a certain consciousness of a different heritage, inherent in geography and climate, whatever the southern-born writer chooses to write about, it will most probably have a touch of regional flavor.

Of course, there will always be a place for the witty, satirical, ironic comedies of manners, like those of Ellen Glasgow and Josephine Pinckney.

The emphasis on children in southern novels and short stories should be remarked, as in James Agee, Peter Taylor, Capote, and Donald Windham; and strikingly in Lee's *To Kill a Mockingbird,* McCuller's *Member of the Wedding,* and in Elise Sanguinetti's refreshing, humorous *The Last of the Whitfields.* They are often bright, precocious, original thinkers and full of personality. Peter Taylor's children are peculiarly sensitive and perceptive.

One factor still strongly persists in southern letters: concern for the individual character and his humanity. Witness the eccentrics, the lovable crazy folk, "the cussedness of human beings." The South is one place left in which an individual may act out his own dramatic improvisations and not give a hoot what people may think.

Even if the South succumbs to the complexities of modern society, there will be for a long time a place for folklore and a fictional reshaping of some significant historical event, like, for instance, the Black Patch Tobacco War (1903-1907), which Borden Deal is now writing about, and the *Landbreakers* of John Ehle, an epic about North Carolina pioneers in the eighteenth century.

History and tradition are still strong in the South, and with some writers there is a brooding nostalgia for the recent, as well as the distant, past. The sense of a former tragedy casting its shadow on the present is still implicit in many southern novels and gives a certain perspective whereby the characters take on more significance and more grandeur. Without that shadow one may get merely something like the rootless, neuter wasteland of modern suburbia.

In regard to the South and its current writing, no region of the hemisphere today is richer in tradition or more actively in flux than the South. None is more flourishing with creative energy and production. I quote what I said to a *Time Magazine* interviewer in 1944: "There is more passion, more sentiment, more violence, more grace, more variety, and more future in the South than in any other section of the nation." This still seems true of southern literature today.

Comments BY WALTER L. SULLIVAN

Let us examine the image of the Renaissance related to the flowering of southern literature, and take up that image and even extend it a little bit. The English Renaissance was a period of change, and, like all periods of social modification, it produced a literary fruition of very high quality. Yet, the sense of change in that society is perhaps more apparent to us as we look back at it than it was to those who lived through it. Undeniably, Shakespeare and his distinguished contemporaries must have felt deeply what was happening in their nation and in the world. Knowing what they did about man and his history, they must have foreseen much of the agony that was coming. But during the Renaissance, England was the most stable nation in the civilized world. While war raged on the continent, there was peace in England. While the countries on the continent suffered severe economic stress, there was prosperity in England. The religious difficulties in Britain during the Renaissance were nothing compared to those that would come a few years later. Even the Guy Fawkes plot to blow up Parliament signified no popular revolutionary spirit, but rather the isolated fanaticism that is found on the fringe of the healthiest societies.

Very soon after the Renaissance came the interregnum; and after the interregnum Dryden, looking back to the writers of Elizabethan days, referred to "that race of giants before the flood." Now, when the interregnum came, and we may now have reached our own spiritual interregnum, there was a general exacerbation of feeling. People who had gotten along well together, and who had contented themselves with executing others only occasionally, now began seriously to attempt to wipe each other out. With the interregnum, there was large agreement that the Establishment in all its particulars was bad, but there was by no means any unified notion of what might be better. You will remember that in 1643, Thomas Edwards set out to catalogue the various religious denominations. He thought he would make a list of the ways in which one could be a Christian. He got through that book, and he saw that while he had been writing, another book-full of denominations had sprung up. He compiled a second volume and then a third; and then with the job still far from complete, he quit in disgust. Edwards' experience was indicative of the splintering that his society was suffering. There was no longer any unity of spirit or of philosophy.

The interregnum saw the rise of scientific thought and the decline of religion which accompanied it. The notion of the Great Chain of Being, on which Shakespeare and his contemporaries had depended for their orderly moral view of the universe, was destroyed. The interregnum saw the destruction of maypoles in England, the debunking of fairy stories, the decline of madrigal singing, in short, the total deterioration of folk culture. The interregnum brought about the hegemony of the Whigs who ruled not according to principle, but according to self interest. It marked the end of the great flowering of English literature. No period like the Renaissance ever came again.

The parallel that I am trying to draw has some validity. What happens when a society gets into a situation like the one we are in now? What happens to society under the circumstances of the interregnum or under our present circumstances? A polarization of opinion, a kind of moral rigidity, results which has a profound effect on what we write. There is in William Faulkner not only an ability to recognize those things about his society that are good and those things about his society that are bad; there is a great capacity to hate the sin, yet also to love the sinner. One of my very favorite characters in Faulkner is Jason Compson as he appears in that remarkable section of *The Sound and the Fury*. Here is a man who is a perfect horror. He is misrepresenting his business affairs to his mother. He is stealing from his niece. He refuses to give Luster the tickets to the traveling show: when Luster is unable to pay him for them, he drops them in the stove. He is rude to Dilsey who is the last remnant of stability in the family. When he loses money on the commodity exchange, he blames the Jews in Chicago. He is failing in business, and he blames this on the Negroes. In both his attitudes and his actions, he is an almost totally deplorable person. And yet, he is a wonderfully human creation, and at the end, you feel a bit sorry for him, Jason Compson though he is.

His money is gone. He stole most of it, to be sure, but the loss is to him severely painful. He has been chasing across the countryside, trying to find Quentin. He has been knocked about in a fight; he is far from home and his automobile is disabled; he has a headache. His world has collapsed, and there can be no question that he deserves what has happened to him. Yet, he is an eminently human figure, and in his humanity, he transcends his paltry self. It is as if Faulkner were saying to us, "This is terrible, but we can survive it. This is a part of the human scene: we are all here together, the good and the bad, and there is something magnificent about all of us."

A literary image which accurately reflects our own time is the Misfit in Flannery O'Connor's "A Good Man Is Hard to Find." The Misfit is a beautifully flat character. He has all the moral angularity of modern man. He is, of course, crazy, but his very insanity is significant in terms of what has happened to us in our own interregnum. In the stiffness of the social and religious and economic positions we take against each other—in our separation from God, as Miss O'Connor would put it—we become dehumanized and grotesque. The Misfit goes through the world amusing himself by the worst sort of criminal activity. You will recall that the vacationing family in that story has an automobile accident and thereby falls into the hands of the Misfit and his helpers. The mother and father and the two children are taken off into the woods and shot by Bobby Lee and Hiram and the grandmother is finally murdered by the Misfit himself. But before he kills the grandmother, he talks to her. "Jesus was the only One that ever raised the dead," he says. "And He shouldn't have done it. He's thrown everything off balance. If He did what He said, then it's nothing for you to do but throw away everything and follow Him, and if He didn't, then it's nothing for you to do but enjoy the few minutes you got left the best way you can—by killing somebody or burning down his house or doing some other meanness to him."

The Misfit seems to be giving us here a kind of irrefutable logic for our time. Caught up as we are in our stern and often violent postures of contradiction, we cannot look at the Jason Compsons of the world and see them for the egregious, sinful, but none the less completely human figures that they are. Rather, like the Misfit, like the people of the English interregnum, like people always when they are under the kind of stress that we are now enduring, we pull off into our various camps. Our views narrow. Our images flatten out. And our literature suffers.